FOLLOW THE ECSTASY

FOLLOW THE ECSTASY

The Hermitage Years of Thomas Merton

John Howard Griffin
Edited by Robert Bonazzi

ORBIS BOOKS

Maryknoll, New York 10545

Library of Congress Cataloging-in-Publication Data

Griffin, John Howard, 1920–
    Follow the ecstacy : the hermitage years of Thomas Merton / John
Howard Griffin ; edited by Robert Bonazzi.
        p.   cm.
    Originally published: Fort Worth, Tex. : JHG Editions/Latitudes
Press, 1983.
    Includes index.
    ISBN 0-88344-847-5 (pbk.)
    1. Merton, Thomas, 1915-1968.   2. Trappists—United States—
Biography.   I. Bonazzi, Robert.   II. Title.
[BX4705.M542G75   1993]
271'.12502—dc20
[B]   92-38710
                                                              CIP

CONTENTS

FOREWORD

Robert Bonazzi

In 1968, the year after Thomas Merton's accidental death by electrocution, John Howard Griffin was invited by the Merton Legacy Trust to write the "official biography" of the Trappist monk and author. The choice seemed providential because Griffin shared remarkable affinities with his friend and colleague.

Besides several retreats at the Abbey of Gethsemani where he met Merton, Griffin had lived in various monasteries, wrote in hermetic solitude and, in his youth, considered the possibility of a monastic vocation. During his initial visit to a cloister, in 1946, he spent a few weeks with the Dominicans, in Paris. This prepared him for a long stay at the Benedictine Abbey of Solesmes that same year and until Easter of 1947. There at the motherhouse of Gregorian Chant, he studied the ancient manuscripts with the monks (who were preeminent musicologists), reached a spiritual awakening under the power of plainsong and the Great Silence from which it emerged, and discovered later the setting of his first novel, *The Devil Rides Outside.* He made regular retreats at the Carmelite monastery near Dallas, Texas during the 1950s when he was blind, becoming a Third Order Carmelite in that decade. In 1957, after regaining his sight, he stayed with the Carmelites to avoid the crush of publicity surrounding this event and to allow his psyche the time to adapt in a restful atmosphere. Following the publication of *Black Like Me*, in 1961, Griffin lectured on racism to thousands in America and Europe, often returning to the solace of the cloister when his tours ended.

Obviously, Merton was a monk and priest whose context was a Cistercian abbey while Griffin, as a family man and a visible public figure, was usually not in a monastery when he read the offices, attended Mass, or prayed. Yet both were Catholic converts, compelled by a quest toward sanctity, highly-disciplined in their solitude, and obedient to the Church even though at times critical of its bureaucratic abuses. With natural humility and intense spirituality, they taught by example and silence. When they did speak of faith it was never to preach with any sense of superiority. Their powerful openness to God led them where others followed, though they sought no honor for themselves but only for God. They shared a great love of the saints—in particular St. Thomas Aquinas and St. John of the Cross—about whom they both wrote.

Merton was the offspring of artistic parents. He showed an early gift for language and visual art, and was deeply influenced by his father's paintings. Griffin's mother, a concert-trained pianist and life-long piano teacher, imbued her son with a passion for classical music.

Born in Prades, Merton was fluent in French (and several other languages), became a significant translator, and wrote poems in French. Although born in Texas, Griffin went to France as a teenager to study at the Lycée Descartes, in Tours. He became the ultimate Francophile, writing his novels in French, translating from that adopted tongue, and developing his skills in French cuisine to a subtly delicious level.

Their conversions were influenced, in part, by the writings of their mutual friends, Jacques and Raïssa Maritain, also converts. Merton translated Raïssa's difficult mystical poems and Griffin published a book about the French philosopher and theologian, *Jacques Maritain: Homage in Words and Pictures*. Merton and Griffin shared also a fascination for such French modernists as Pierre Reverdy, René Char, George Braque, Georges Rouault, François Poulenc, and Albert Camus, writing about the art and aesthetics of these twentieth-century masters.

Merton was a painter who became a photographer in his last years. Several of the monk's miniature abstracts, influenced by Franz Kline's large abstract expressionist canvases, were published in his *Raids on the Unspeakable*, along with a text about his approach to painting. Griffin wrote about Merton's painting and photography in *A Hidden Wholeness: The Visual World of Thomas Merton*. Griffin had a decisive influence on his friend's photography, lending Merton an excellent camera and, with the help of his younger son (Gregory Griffin), developing the monk's prints. Griffin was both a professional photographer and musicologist. He was known internationally for his black and white portraits of Merton, Maritain, Reverdy, and many famous musicians. As a musicologist, he specialized in Gregorian Chant, which had a deep significance for both men.

Both writers kept regular journals over many decades—ongoing, open texts, combining deeply personal meditations, aesthetic analyses, literary seeds, and the political news of the day. Merton's journals, which he excerpted and revised for *The Sign of Jonas*, *Conjectures of a Guilty Bystander*, and *A Vow of Conversation*, will begin appearing in their entirety, in 1994, under the general editorship of Brother Patrick Hart of Gethsemani. Griffin's journals, kept from 1950 until his death in 1980, were excerpted and revised for such books as *The Hermitage Journals, The John Howard Griffin Reader,* and the book on Maritain. *Black Like Me,* Griffin's 1959 encounter with racism in the Deep South, is one of the most widely read journals of this century. Natural diarists, even their published fiction used the form—Merton's *My Argument with the Gestapo* and Griffin's *The Devil Rides Outside.*

Griffin and Merton became significant voices in the critical dialogues of their day regarding human rights, racism, war and peace, spiritual renewal, charitable love in a climate of hatred, and the survival of the environment. They attacked cultural stereotypes, technological icons, political oppression, mass media massage, and stupidity in general. They combined sophisticated discourse, ethical judgment, and personal insight into a vision that vibrated with hope against absurdity. They shared a keen perspective that allowed for radical innovations in the larger context of tradition. They were open to the processes of social and interior change, scrutinizing both the images and realities of society and self. They continued to grow beyond the superficial contradictions of their points of view, always in quest of universal truths that might ignite the fires of justice and, simultaneously, calm the ego with profound humility.

Their work made them controversial figures, but their true vocation to solitude and creativity, to contemplation and prayer, never waned — despite social crises, critical indignation from various quarters, voluminous correspondences, and poor health. Each artist endured fame and suffered from his "public image."

Reflecting on these issues, Griffin wrote of Merton's struggle.

Paradoxically, Merton's very search to be true to a way of life that rendered many ambitions futile, and fame the most futile of all, brought him fame. Aside from his great communicative gifts, Merton's writings coincided with a period in history — the years following the anguish of World War II — when many were confused, bewildered and searching for something better than religious platitudes. Also, Merton's extraordinary personality permeated his works. To understand anything about this personality, popular pietistic images about contemplatives have to be discarded. Merton was a mystic and a poet, with the ability to see many facets of the same object and to combine within himself seeming opposites. He was simultaneously a man of profound discipline and astonishing freedom; a man who expressed himself eloquently concerning the spiritual life but who kept his own secret prayer private; a man of profound religious abandonment who refused to veil his humanity in the gauze of pietism; a man of the intellect who relished the simplest manual labor. He combined strength and toughness with a faultless courtesy toward others. He possessed a high sense of humor and showed great warmth in his relations with others, but had no time to waste on what he called "silliness" and "foolishness" and could terminate such encounters with masterful tact. He would not wear religious masks or pretend, for anyone's edification, to be other than what he was: a man whose interior life was not for display and who was not going to act out anyone else's version of what a contemplative should be.

(*A Hidden Wholeness: The Visual World of Thomas Merton,* 1970)

The previous passage evokes not only Merton, but suggests a self-portrait of Griffin as well. True, this reflection is imprecise in some details, yet it is resonant with artistic affinities and spiritual essences. While Griffin did not compose poems, his prose was poetic. Even though he did not achieve the hermit's prolonged depth of contemplation, he shared the mystical vision. Like Merton, he was eloquent about spirituality but private about his own prayer. Courteous and warm toward others, Griffin was tough on pious and self-serving hypocrites. Blessed with elegant wit and manners, he could be uproariously satirical about his detractors (especially "good white liberals" who felt he was pushing "equality" for black people with reckless abandon), and he was delightfully bawdy when he had to suffer prudes.

Fame followed Merton into the cloister, but Griffin came face to face with this cultural delusion during an intensely public existence. Yet he had always considered the activist role to be alien to his nature.

> I have had a life that I loathe for these past years—I mean the public life. I have had to go in conscience and also because I am under spiritual direction and because we've had one racial crisis after another. I have been able to function in those crises, but all that time I have been away from my desk, away from what my true vocation is. It was only with the awareness that there were people like Merton who didn't have to be in those alleys which gave me the strength to do it. Otherwise I couldn't have done it. I knew he was back there doing what I wished I could be doing.
>
> (Interview with Robert Bonazzi, *Latitudes,* 1967)

With the invitation to write the "official biography" of Merton, Griffin had a valid reason for declining the incessant requests to lecture and write on race relations or to mediate racial crises. Greatly relieved by the chance to embark upon a long-term creative project, he considered the invitation no less than a magnificent calling from God.

As with all his encounters, Griffin approached the world of Thomas Merton by immersing his own being entirely in its reality. By this natural creative method, experience was not deformed by intellectual concepts or by the prejudices of ego. Rather, Griffin held the innocent belief that obvious contradictions—and even mysteries—might be clarified by the slightest movement of grace.

In this spirit, he kept a journal while living in the monk's hermitage for 168 days—from August of 1969 until June of 1972. The result was *The Hermitage Journals: A Diary Kept While Working on the Biography of Thomas Merton*—Griffin's last completed book, intended as a companion to his "official biography," which was left unfinished. Both *The Hermitage Journals* and *Follow the Ecstasy* were published posthumously, in 1981 and 1983 respectively. Along with *A Hidden Wholeness*, they form a trilogy, and stand as an integral part of Griffin's overall search for the essential Merton.

Even though *Follow the Ecstasy* is the unpolished portion of an unfinished work, it holds several unique illuminations. The text draws on the monk's private journals, which Griffin considered the key to understanding Merton. He was the first scholar to have access to these pages and they were the object of his contemplation for eight years. While Michael Mott had this same access later, it is clear from his "Official Biography," *The Seven Mountains of Thomas Merton*, that he did not view these journals as his central guide, nor did he read them with Griffin's intuitive perspective of solitude. Mott's study is an invaluable sourcebook for every Merton scholar, as well as an accurate account of the monk's life for the general reader, but it is mainly a book of facts and scholarly interpretations from which the essential Merton does not emerge. The difference lies in the reality of solitude as opposed to its many surface images. Writing about Merton, Griffin clarifies this distinction in *Follow the Ecstasy*.

He loved the loneliness of the night. It taught him to view solitude as act, and to conclude that the reason no one really understood solitude was because men viewed it as a condition, something one elected to undergo — like standing under a shower. Actually, solitude was for him a realization; even a kind of creation as well as a liberation of active forces within him. As a mere condition, solitude could be passive, inert and basically unreal: a kind of coma. To avoid this condition, he had to work actively at solitude.

Thus, the need for discipline, for techniques of integration that keep body and soul together, harmonizing their powers to bring them into one deep resonance oriented to the root of being.

Freedom began for Fr. Louis with the willingness to realize and experience his life as totally absurd in relation to the apparent meaning which had been thrown over life by society and by illusions. But that could be only a starting point leading to a deeper realization of that root reality in himself and in all life *"which I do not know and cannot know. . . .* This implies the capacity to see that *realizing* and *knowing* are not the same . . . solitude itself is the fullness of realization. In solitude I become *fully able to realize what I cannot know."*

This sort of synthesis combines Griffin's own involvement with solitude at the hermitage and his empathetic reading of Merton's private reflections. It is not intellectual analysis, fixing parameters of a concept, but the provisional articulation of a process.

When Griffin first came to live in the hermitage, he felt a "forlorn kind of terror at the immensity of the solitude," because he still carried "the nerve-seeped smog of the cities." Later in *The Hermitage Journals*, as he was absorbed by the natural sounds of the woods and his own attentive silence, Griffin felt "bewilderment that God should flood me with such fine gifts, and I utter prayers of thanksgiving for Tom for being the instrument that brought me here to where Christ obviously wanted to find me. ...." In that solitude, there was no need to search for anything or anyone, "because there in the surrounding silence all that would otherwise be loneliness is filled with Christ, filled with that ravishment." This primary illumination of *Follow the Ecstasy* is—simultaneously—an evocation of the immediate environment, an intimate reading of the monk's private journals, and an experiential anatomy of solitude.

Next, there is an illumination of a different kind. In Griffin's objective portrayal, the reader encounters an extraordinary surprise in the life of this famous monk (who was also a priest and the first Cistercian hermit since the Middle Ages): A love story, and this was not just the most significant love story we would expect to find—the soul's adoration of God—but one involving human affection. In 1966, Thomas Merton shared a romantic relationship with a young nurse who cared for him during his stay in a Louisville hospital for back surgery. The woman, who is called "S" in Mott's "Official Biography" and unnamed in other Merton studies, was Margie Smith. Griffin was the first writer to tell this story which Merton had recorded in his journals, two unpublished notebooks, as well as indirectly in a limited edition of poems (*18 Poems*), posthumously published by New Directions, in 1985.

For Griffin, a man devoted to the integrity of privacy, this was a difficult decision. How to tell the truth as Merton had told it without sensationalism and to avoid damaging Margie Smith's own right to privacy? In an extended series of dialogues with James Laughlin (Merton's longtime friend and publisher at New Directions, who was also one of the three trustees of the Merton Legacy Trust) and Father Flavian Burns (Merton's Abbot at Gethsemani and a valued friend of the monk), Griffin weighed every aspect of the question. During that same period, Margie Smith was in correspondence with Laughlin, and she made no objections to Griffin writing an interpretation of the facts. By that time, she had moved to another part of the country and was sharing a happy life with her new husband.

With the counsel and encouragement of Margie Smith, James Laughlin, and Abbot Flavian Burns, Griffin completed the 1966 chapter, achieving a clear perspective that all viewed with approval. Throughout the entire discourse there had been only one goal, a goal hoped for in the private writings of Merton himself: that the truth be told. This was accomplished.

Griffin summarized that truth most succinctly in *Follow the Ecstasy*:

Although Merton was tormented by this period of profound emotional attachment, ultimately the experience confirmed for him what had before been intuitive conclusions. He could now know that his profoundest statements about love between two human beings held equally true about love between man and God, and that he himself had the capacity to love fully. Since he had never, during this experience, seriously questioned the validity of his vocation, the experience itself verified what he had intuited. His vocation consisted in the total gift of himself to God and through God to man. He now knew that he possessed an authentic potential for love and that his religious committment was not the subtle disguise of an emotional cripple. This provided an inner liberation which gave him a new sense of sureness, uncautiousness, defenselessness in his vocation and in the depths of himself.

Near the end of 1966, Merton decided to take the steps necessary for securing his private journals from public attention until twenty-five years after his death. However, according to Griffin, the monk had no intention of suppressing the truth about his attachment to Margie Smith. In fact, his deepest concern was for her feelings and privacy. "I have always wanted to be completely open," Merton wrote in his journal, "both about my mistakes and about my efforts to make sense out of my life." He had summed up his spiritual friendship with Margie Smith in one word: "devotion." He viewed the relationship as a significant part of the entire picture, because it revealed his "limitations as well as a side of me that is—well, it needs to be known, too, for it is a part of me. My need for love, my inner division, the struggle in which solitude is at once a problem and a solution."

A third aspect illuminating *Follow the Ecstasy* is Griffin's personal portrait of the monk found in the Prologue and Epilogue. These texts, commissioned by anthologists for published collections about Merton, were not specifically intended by the author for inclusion in his biography. However, there is no doubt in this editor's mind that Griffin would have written a first-person preface to what was intended as a highly objective biography. Since this material was available in complete form, and because it sheds an intimate light upon the Merton-Griffin friendship, it was included. Both authors were deeply autobiographical, and even when their books were not exclusively personal, it was natural for them to preface those texts with some private words.

The Prologue—an essay reprinted from the Summer 1969 issue of *Continuum*—was originally entitled "Les Grandes Amitiés" by Griffin, a deliberate echo of Raïssa Maritain's reminiscence of the same name. Peter Kountz, a Merton scholar, made some astute observations about Griffin's Prologue and its original title in a review of *Follow the Ecstasy.*

The title of the piece (Griffin's first published work on the monk) is quite deliberately chosen, for it is the account of the "great friendships" between two men. Griffin must have been careful to use the plural of *amitié*—a word that can be understood as friendship, kindness, or complement—for his essay reveals that their friendship was not simply *one* friendship but a many-layered set of intimacies based on a remarkable mutual kindness and respect. Using *amitié* in yet another way, the essay reveals that each man complements the other

by allowing each to be himself. Here are two men, friends and colleagues, who are forever letting one another be in writing, in photography, and face-to-face. Here are two men forever saying goodbye
because they are so wary of intruding, so wary of violating one another's sensibilities. We see this so clearly in Griffin's account of Merton's
growing passion for photography. Griffin is quick to recognize that
Merton is no ordinary photographer. "The passion was simply another
means for expressing his vision: the challenge to capture on film something of the solitude and silence and essences that preocccupied him."
And how remarkable it is that John Howard Griffin, himself a "Master
Photographer," did not tamper with these early signs of Merton's gift
or with Merton's own way of photography. He could have. He was
ever faithful to "Les Grandes Amitiés."

("On John Howard Griffin on Merton," *Kairos*, 1988)

Griffin and Merton shared a fraternal dialogue — a symbiotic exchange
of speech and silence — which was never a dual monologue. When one spoke
the other listened without cluttering the mind with the next response. Once
it became apparent that real resolution was beyond articulation, they fell
silent, left the mystery in God's hands, and usually went on another jaunt
through Gethsemani's woods to photograph the objects of their contemplation. This brief Prologue tells the delightful tale of two gifted artists
equally at ease during innocent adventures and serious conversations. And
it is an intimate portrait, resonating with sensitivity and charm, true to
Merton and worthy of the vintage Griffin prose style.

The Epilogue is a compilation of Griffin's unpublished notes woven into
a portion of his article, "The Controversial Merton," which appeared in
the 1978 Paulist Press anthology, *Thomas Merton: Prophet in the Belly of a
Paradox*. This final section is a brief overview of the main themes in Merton's later work that stirred controversy. It also discloses a few of Griffin's
most intuitive perceptions about his friend.

Had Thomas Merton returned from the East alive, he would have
become more and more silent. He would have gone on writing forever — for he was a true poet as well as a faithful monk and priest —
but he would have published less and less. He would have continued
taking the authentic risks necessary to live his vocation without compromise. He had lived in an absolute way. This is courageous because
he had every chance for taking the easy way out. He never did. He
never wavered from his true vocation: to be always leaping over the
cliffs of the spiritual life.

It was characteristic of John Howard Griffin to write a first draft swiftly,
then to revise a manuscript incessantly until a final text was achieved. He
rarely showed portions of his work-in-progress to anyone and never reread

his books once they were published. *Follow the Ecstasy* is an exception to this method because the composition was slowed by years of meticulous research and interrupted by the debilitating effects of diabetes. Although Griffin worked a decade on the project, only the chapters on Merton's final years (and several other scattered chapters) were left in nearly-complete form. Because this "hermitage" period most fascinated Griffin and it was the freshest in the memories of the witnesses he interviewed, he wrote it first. But even this portion remained in second draft, undoubtedly less polished than he would have made it had he been able. Deeply disappointed by his failing energy, Griffin reluctantly turned the project back to his publisher, and a second official biographer was appointed.

Nonetheless, *Follow the Ecstasy: The Hermitage Years of Thomas Merton* is a highly readable account, offering many diamonds in the rough — soulful, translucent gems that do not call for further polishing, only contemplation.

This leaves one other point to contemplate. Generally, Griffin labored over his book titles, eventually finding evocative and memorable ones: *Black Like Me* from a Langston Hughes poem; *The Devil Rides Outside* after a French proverb; and two titles quoted from the work of Thomas Merton — *A Hidden Wholeness* (a line in one of the monk's prose poems, "Hagia Sophia") and *A Time to Be Human* (from his translation of Chuang Tzu). However, Griffin left no title for this account of Merton's hermitage years.

When Latitudes Press and the Griffin Estate joined forces to publish the first edition, *Follow the Ecstasy* became the title, and Merton's poems were added to the text. The title is based on a remark made to Merton by Nicanor Parra during their 1966 visit. In a review of the first edition, Carin Dunne highlighted the paradox suggested by the encounter: "At one point the Chilean poet, Nicanor Parra, advised Merton to "follow the ecstasy." Does it mean to go with the passion, abandoning a path to which he had avowed himself? Or is it an invitation to a more permanent *ecstasis*, a release from selfishness and self-centeredness?" While the intent of Parra's remark remains a mystery, Merton's actions answer Dunne's thoughtful musings. The monk offered himself in utter humility to the grace of God, and he was delivered beyond all human concerns.

This new Orbis edition arrives in the year that marks the twenty-fifth anniversary of Thomas Merton's death in 1968. Brother Patrick Hart, the monk's former secretary and one of the world's significant Merton scholars, has made this observation more poignantly. He calls 1993 "the twenty-fifth anniversary of Merton's passage through death to life."

Certainly the beloved monk lives in Griffin's pages and in his magnificent photographs we see added to this edition. Griffin's vision of his brother in Christ incarnate an intense presence, and we are given a rare gift from two lives of pure giving.

FOLLOW THE ECSTASY

PROLOGUE

I am in a condition of ecstasy over the human race.
— Thomas Merton

We had read one another's books. We knew something about one another long before my first visit to Gethsemani. On that first visit, I went simply to spend a few days in a Trappist silence, to follow the office, to be alone.

A number of the family brothers and the guestmaster asked if I would not be seeing Father Louis (Thomas Merton's name in religion) and expressed mild surprise that I had made no arrangements to meet him. Indeed, they expressed a kind of generous fraternal regret that we would not meet. I told them that I would of course, love to meet him, to shake his hand. But I did not wish to disturb his solitude by any intrusion.

We did meet briefly. Word got to him that I was there. We shook hands; he gave me a book he had signed for me. I explained to him why I had not written to ask for permission to see him. He expressed appreciation, quite simply and frankly, that I had not. We talked quickly about mutual friends — Dom Bede Griffiths, Jacques and Raïssa Maritain. He moved to leave and then returned to tell me, "If you have the chance to come here again, don't write the Father Abbot for permission to see me. It works better if you write me and then I'll ask for permission to see you."

The entire visit lasted only a few minutes, but we had no barriers to get out of the way, no need to "come to know one another." We met as old friends, and quite especially as colleagues.

A few weeks later I was invited back by Father Abbot James Fox, whom I had met on my first visit. He said he knew that I was involved in exhausting work and he hoped I would feel free to come there just to rest any time I felt the need.

I wrote him and Thomas Merton that for many years I had been building a private archive of photographs of men and women, famous and unknown, in their typical activities. I had done this with Jacques Maritain and with Dominique Pire, and I wrote that I would like very much, without any intention of publishing, to do this with Thomas Merton. Permission was given. Father Abbot, in fact, said that they would like to have a contemporary portrait of Thomas Merton, an "official" one they could release to replace those made in Merton's youth that were still being used in news-

1

papers and magazines. We agreed that I would photograph freely and without restrictions, but that no photograph would be released without my written consent and the abbey's.

When I arrived for the photographic session I was gratified to see that Thomas Merton had made no special preparation. He wore his habit, a blue denim jacket and a knitted black wool cap. A slight stubble of whiskers marked his chin. He suggested that we go up to the hermitage and I quickly agreed. He explained that he was not living there yet but hoped to move in completely in the future. He spent some of his days on the mountain top working in the concrete block house.

We climbed the hill. He talked but I could not answer because my lungs were not accustomed to such strenuous activity. When we arrived at the hermitage, my hands shook so badly I could not work and I could speak only in gasps.

Tom sat me down on the edge of the porch in a clear cold sunlight so I could recover from the climb while he went to fetch wood for the fireplace.

I rested in the silence of that isolated place and watched him make trips to the woodpile, load his arms with firewood and carry it inside. In twenty minutes my trembling had stopped and I began to smell the fragrance of wood smoke from the chimney. Tom came out to see if I were sufficiently recovered to walk inside. We dubbed the climb "heart attack hill" and I promised him I would never attempt to walk it again — at least not at the pace he set.

Tom explained rather apologetically that the hermitage was not as "poor" as it should be, but that it had been built as a conference room, a place for discussions with visiting groups. Though handsome, with no electricity and no water the hermitage seemed appropriately "poor" to me. The morning sun, reflecting from the stone floor and walls, filled the room with a soft brilliance ideal for photography.

I began to prepare my cameras on the long work-table near the window. Tom showed no stiffening. Would he, like so many subjects, have masks that a photographer has to penetrate before photographing the person?

"May I begin shooting?" I asked.

"Sure. What do you want me to do?"

"Just whatever you would do if I weren't here. Read, write, tend the fire, anything so long as you pay no attention to me."

I began to shoot frames to accustom him to the sight and sound of the camera. We talked easily. No problems about his assuming any poses. He was perfectly natural. He was rare in this, utterly unconcerned about his "image." He retained the denim jacket and wool cap until the fire warmed the room.

Though Tom didn't wear masks, I had other problems. His face concealed nothing. It changed every moment, swiftly, with changes in his thoughts or moods. How to catch all of that? How to capture what was truly characteristic? He was up, down, grabbing books to show me things as new topics for discussion were introduced. We talked of Victor Hammer, his old friend, and Tom showed me the things Victor had made for him. I mentioned Victor's chapel at Kolbsheim—the one he had designed and built for the Gruneliuses. I had visited it. Tom had photographs of it.

We talked photography. He knew nothing about it, but he was fascinated by what I was doing. He was amused when I told him of the tendency of very intelligent men to freeze up and become unnatural the moment the lens was pointed at them. I told him of Jacques Maritain's discomfort, the first few times I photographed him, at what he called my "machine-gunning."

"Most people are like that," I said. "You and Pierre Reverdy are the two easiest to photograph."

In that day's photographing and talking I became aware of a quality that was to characterize all our subsequent meetings—an unblemished happiness with the moment, a concentration on the moment, as though there were no yesterday or tomorrow. It was like the experience of music, each moment felicitous, enough in itself. This is rare in human contacts, I think.

Tom was a man of enlightened pessimism about the world. Many of our meetings left us with the feeling that this country was moving toward ever increasing sacrifice of the freedoms we professed to uphold. But even with such a depressing prognosis, his natural buoyancy, his robust humor and his grasp of the absurd made the most pessimistic meetings happy ones. He demonstrated a completely selfless capacity for affection that freed his friends from the need to role-play or to be anything except what they were. His friendship demanded nothing—it did not seek to dominate or possess or convert or in any way alter another—and rarely judged. He created an atmosphere of such reality that his friends were freed from any need to "be careful" in his presence out of fear of introducing some jarring note. Any deliberate or contrived attitude of pietistic "high-mindedness" would have appeared utterly false in his presence. So meetings with him had a kind of joy that remained untainted no matter what else might be happening around us.

Our relationship took on a comic quality in our attempts to say good-bye forever. Every time we were together we parted with the intention of not seeing one another again. He had a vocation for the solitary life, the life of silence and contemplation and creativity. Nothing is less compatible with the quality of solitude he needed than visits from friends. Only after his death did we realize the enormous demands that were made on his solitude by individuals who did not, of course, realize how many other individuals sought his time and attention.

How often did I write him: "I will consider it a failure of my friendship for you if I ever hear from you again. Please do not take the time from your life to write to me."

He would agree, but ask me to continue faithfully sending him material. "You once said you were astounded that a white man could have such perception of the problems of black men," he wrote. "If that is so it is because friends like you keep me informed." So it was agreed that I would send him whatever I thought important, but that he would not answer me.

On each visit to Gethsemani, I wrote him that I was coming but that I would not ask to see him since there was no need for any personal contact. Invariably our paths would cross at the abbey, or he would come to my room, and we would visit as though it were for the last time, with that special flavor of a few moments together that we had not anticipated we would have.

Finally, when he moved to the mountain-top hermitage, he wrote with great happiness that all visits would cease, that his mail would be curtailed, that he would have true solitude. I wrote him that I was overjoyed. At last he would have the silence and solitude that had been so often interrupted.

For months I heard nothing more from him, and I supposed that I would never hear from him again. I was deeply happy for him. Occasionally I would get a mimeographed poem or article he had written, with a few words written in his hand on the title page. Then he sent me some photographs he had made of roots with an Instamatic camera. He wrote a letter, explaining that his interest in photography had grown, and he wondered if I could make some prints in my darkroom. I made the prints he wanted, sent them back with high praise, and asked him to call on me for any future such service.

I began to learn of his life there in the hermitage through the writings and drawings he sent me. His energies flowed in all directions—in his writing, in his calligraphy, his occasional photography whenever he could borrow a camera. I knew that he chopped his wood and gathered it for the fireplace.

In 1966 I received a letter from Jacques Maritain saying he had heard that Tom was having some back problems and was in a hospital in Louisville for surgery. Jacques asked me to get all the details and write him immediately.

When I telephoned the abbey, Father Abbot Fox suggested I could get more precise information from the hospital and gave me the number to call.

After some explaining, the hospital asked if I would like to speak directly with Tom.

"Do you mean that's possible?" I asked.

"I think we can plug a phone in his room."

Some minutes later I heard his voice, jovial and full of enthusiasm. We cleared away the details of his illness and then he asked me how I was fixed for money.

"I'm all right," I said, wondering if he needed money. "Why?"

"If you're flush, then let's talk a long time," he suggested. Since we had never anticipated talking to one another again, this was too good an opportunity to miss.

We talked. I told him about our new daughter, Amanda, that Jacques Maritain was the godfather, and that he was coming to visit us in a few weeks. "But please, don't tell anyone, Tom," I said. "He doesn't want anyone to know he's coming—he's afraid the TV and press will pester him."

"Couldn't you bring him to Gethsemani to see me," Tom asked. "It'll probably be the last chance we'll have to see each other."

"It will be," I said. "He doesn't plan any more trips to the U.S. But I thought you were never going to see anyone again. Jacques would hesitate to disturb your solitude, just as I would."

"Oh, but something like that—a chance to see Jacques once more."

"Are you sure it would be all right? Won't you have to get permission from Father Abbot? I don't want to suggest it to Jacques until it is cleared with the abbot. No sense building up Jacques' hopes for a reunion and then . . ."

Tom assured me that Father Abbot would be happy to receive him.

Almost immediately I received an airmail letter from Father Abbot Fox urging me to bring Jacques there for a visit.

Our meeting at Gethsemani turned into a magnificent reunion of old friends. Penn Jones and Babeth Manuel accompanied us because I was in a wheelchair and Jacques had become so frail. We needed help getting around. At the abbey we met other friends who had come to see Jacques and Tom—Father J. Stanley Murphy, C.S.B., from Canada, and Dan Walsh, the philosopher.

For Jacques and Tom the meeting had a special autumnal significance. Tom held Raïssa Maritain in special esteem, the love of a poet for a poet. She had died in 1960, a few weeks after the death of Pierre Reverdy.

After supper and a bull session the night of our arrival, we retired early in order to begin the next day at dawn, with Mass celebrated by Tom. Afterward, Penn Jones drove us up the hill to Tom's hermitage. The air was still chilled. Tom had risen much earlier and had warmed the room with a fire in the fireplace. We arrived an hour after sunrise, went inside and sat around the fireplace to talk. The topics were unimportant. We were simply aware of an overwhelming joy at being together in that time and place, surrounded by the woods, the isolation, the brilliance of sunlight in autumn. All enthusiasms were heightened by the rarity of it. I photographed endlessly, not only to capture the hours, but because the excitement made us feel that exaggeration was the right and normal emotion. Where ten shots would have sufficed under ordinary conditions, a thousand seemed appropriate for the jubilance of the light and of our feelings.

Tom was everywhere doing everything. To save Jacques from the fatigue of English, Tom spoke only French with his old friend. They discussed mutual acquaintances, their work—Tom was preparing a study of the poetry and songs of Bob Dylan, "the American Villon," as he described him. Tom put on some recordings of Dylan's songs so Jacques would know what he was talking about. Played at full volume, the Dylan songs blasted the still atmosphere of Trappist lands with the "wang-wang" of guitar and voice at high amplification. He prepared coffee for us in the two cups he possessed and saw to our needs, expressing an energy that seemed electric, but with no loss of calm.

After a while Jacques and Tom came to a discussion of Tom's new life, his new work. Tom told him about it, and added, "As for the spiritual life, I don't worry about it. It just takes care of itself."

Jacques looked happily at him and nodded approvingly.

As I photographed more and more, Tom began to inch toward me and my cameras. Finally he came and asked about them. I explained that one was a Leica, and the other an Alpa, the same instrument that David Douglas Duncan had used in his reproduction of Picasso's paintings in *Picasso's Picassos.*

I handed it to him, watched him handle it as though it were a precious jewel.

"Would you like to use it today?" I asked.

It was like placing a concert grand piano at the disposal of a gifted musician who had never played on anything but an upright. Tom began to shoot as freely as I had been and always afterward he referred to that "Picasso camera."

A passion for photography of a special kind had been building in Tom. He had no interest whatsoever in ordinary photography; the passion was simply for another means for expressing his vision, the challenge to capture on film something of the solitude and silence and essences that preoccupied him.

As always in my association with him, this interest began to bend the day to its needs. By afternoon, when we went out into the woods and sat at the edge of a lake, Tom talked mostly with the camera at his eye, looking at the world, at leaves and trees and the reflections of water through the ground-glass viewfinder. It was fascinating to see a man who knew little or nothing of photography working with great speed and energy toward doing something with photography that he had never seen done before. The camera became in his hands, almost immediately, an instrument of contemplation—at least potentially—and it remained that for him until his death, which explains why he became not only a gifted but a uniquely original photographer. He himself later distinguished between his "documentary" photography of places, people and events, and his "serious" work. He was never terribly interested in the former. He was profoundly immersed in the latter. In the last two years of his life, although he had rarely "achieved" what he was seeking photographically, he spent a great deal of his time working toward it, doing studies with the camera.

We said our final good-bye when we left after this reunion. Tom would go back into solitude, see no one except under extraordinary circumstances in the future. He asked me to continue sending him any materials dealing especially with civil rights. He embraced Jacques and me and we left him.

Of course, there was the necessary correspondence. We processed the rolls of film Tom had taken at the reunion, and this required some personal as well as technical mail. When that was finished and we had said good-bye again, a few weeks passed in silence.

Then I received a letter from him. He had continued his photographing, borrowing cameras where and when he could. He photographed natural forms—the roots of trees, leaves, branches. In this letter, Tom said that the drugstore processing he had been using did not give him the quality he had hoped for and asked if my son, Gregory, could do his darkroom work.

Gregory accepted with enthusiasm.

The films began to come in—all sizes, all formats, depending on what camera Tom had borrowed. They ranged from superb negatives made with a Rolleiflex to miserable ones made on dollar cameras, where little of the detail Tom wanted had been captured because of the cheap lenses.

Then I wrote and suggested that he would never have much satisfaction until he got himself a good camera that he could learn to know intimately and handle consistently.

He answered that although his pictures were beginning to sell for book jackets, he did have some poverty obligations and did not want to ask for permission to buy such a camera, especially when he was not sure just how deeply he wanted to become involved with photography.

From my point of view, he was showing great gifts and I regretted every negative that was rendered useless because of a poor camera he had used. I felt that something was being lost or jeopardized—an authentic part of his vision. Finally I simply sent him the proper equipment "on perpetual loan."

I asked him to send a card if the instruments arrived safely.

I received no card, but a letter saying that one of the most joy-filled days of his memory occurred when that box arrived. He had opened it, studied the camera, "a beautiful instrument." He looked through the viewfinder and 50mm lens, and then attached the 100mm lens. "When I looked through that, it just blew my mind," he wrote. He then explained that he was going to make provision immediately that when he died all this equipment should be returned to me.

I did not take him seriously, of course, since he was so full of vitality and neither of us, I think, had any notion except that he would outlive me by a hundred or so years. I naturally never expected to see the camera and lenses again, and did not want to. I was interested only in making sure that this greatly gifted man had the means of expressing a gift that I perceived as a photographer.

From then on photography overwhelmed our other interests. A constant stream of film poured into our darkroom to be processed. We stopped saying good-bye—it had gotten to be embarrassing. We corresponded constantly about his work; we would send him contact sheets, he would mark a few, ask for enlargements, we would send the enlargements, then discuss them by letter.

When I went to Gethsemani, we would get together to discuss other things—civil rights, the church, and Vietnam. But after the briefest time, we would abandon that and discuss his pictures, his contact sheets, and end up with our cameras on a photographic jaunt into the woods, or through the cloister.

On my last visit, shortly before his departure for Asia, I went particularly to have a session with him concerning my book *The Church and the Black Man.* We talked about this for a few minutes, and fell into a depression about some of the things that were happening. Our conversation frittered off into talk about the Black Priests Caucus, and the poor response it had received. We got gloomier and gloomier.

Tom was sitting in my room, slumped down in a chair, looking at his hands. A silence settled between us. We had accomplished nothing.

"We're not going to solve this. It's beyond human solution now. It's in God's hands," he said. "Do you feel like going out and photographing?"

The gloom was instantly replaced. We got into the rented car I had brought and drove up to the hermitage. He grabbed his camera and film and directed me toward an old whiskey plant nearby.

We photographed everything—the peeling paint on window facings of abandoned buildings, plants, weeds, rusting railroad cars, a stack of wood-chips. He would see something in the distance, wander away to photograph it from all angles. From a distance he would yell that he had found something interesting. I marveled at his vigor and enthusiasm. Every time he became absorbed, I would photograph him photographing. I did not know that he did the same with me. Once I turned with my camera at my eye to find him aiming at me with his camera. He lowered it briefly and I photographed him. Then I lowered mine and he photographed me.

A sudden downpour drove us back to the abbey. I stopped on the way to let him off at the hermitage. We said good-bye and I watched him through the rain-pocked windows of the car as he hurried into the hermitage, his jean-clad stocky figure bent almost double over the camera to protect it from the rain.

During the months he was away on the trip to Asia, he sent films to be processed and letters. "If the curry doesn't get me, I'll be in Bangkok next week," and "The trip would be unbearable if I could not find time and place to read and meditate. I've had good luck with this," and "I suppose I'll need copies of all these Asian photos as a kind of documentation of the trip." I sensed he did not have the enthusiasm for this "documentation" in photography that he had for the more personal "serious" photography.

On December 11 we received news of Merton's death in Bangkok on the tenth. I returned to Gethsemani on the day of the funeral, December 17, and closed my photographic archives with some shots the next morning of the red clay mound of his grave beneath a large cypress tree in the monastic graveyard.

Father August Thompson, a black priest from Louisiana, stood praying at the grave. An overcast and somber sky appeared to increase and finally fuse our emotions of sadness into serenity and even gladness and relief for Tom that he was now where his life had prepared him to be.

It seemed over then, but even that good-bye was not final. On learning that his camera would be returned with his effects, I wrote and pleaded that the camera not be opened by customs or anyone else. There might be exposed film in it.

Weeks later the camera and extra lens arrived, carefully packaged and wrapped. I tried to open it, but my hands trembled so uncontrollably my wife had to finish the job.

I was overwhelmed to see how immaculately Tom had cared for the equipment—the body and lenses were spotless. I glanced at the frame counter and saw that eighteen shots had been taken of the roll then in the camera body.

More carefully than I have ever done anything in my life, I removed that roll of film and held it in my hand, realizing that on eighteen frames were undeveloped images of scenes Tom had been the last to see when he clicked the shutter and I would be the first to see when they assumed form and detail in the developer. What had registered in his brain and senses, what had interested him, existed latent in that undeveloped emulsion.

I mixed all fresh chemicals and worked with care. Rarely have such tensions cluttered the small space of my darkroom. If these negatives were ruined or spotted or scratched, they could never be replaced. These scenes could never again be photographed with the special vision of Thomas Merton, never again composed and captured with the whole culture of Thomas Merton.

I began to breathe again when finally I held the strip of dripping negatives to the light and saw good clean images.

When they were dry, I put the strip into the enlarger, selected one of the last images at random, focussed and exposed it on photographic paper.

Moments later I held the enlarged photograph in my hands. I looked through Tom's eyes on a scene viewed from some high place, downward past an edge of building and a foreground of shore across a broad body of water from which reflected sunlight glinted back into the viewer's eyes—a kind of universal all-embracing view of men and boats and water seen from the perspective of height and distance.

Only later did a friend, Irving Sussman, unaware of this photograph, point out the prophetic nature of Tom's preoccupation with his own death in *Conjectures of a Guilty Bystander,* written five years before his death. His words, "I think sometimes that I may soon die, though I am not yet old (forty-seven)" mingled with the description of a dream about "walking 'toward the center' without quite knowing where I was going. Suddenly I came to a dead end, but on a height, looking at a great bay, an arm of the harbor" (pp. 170-72).

1965

—— ❖ ——

A Messenger from the Horizon

Look, a naked runner
A messenger,
Following the wind
From budding hills.

By sweet sunstroke
Wounded and signed,
(He is therefore sacred)
Silence is his way.

Rain is his own
Most private weather.
Amazement is his star.

O stranger, our early hope
Flies fast by,
A mute comet, an empty sun.
Adam is his name!

O primeval angel
Virgin brother of astonishment,
Born of one word, one bare
Inquisitive diamond.

O blessed
Invulnerable cry,
O unplanned Saturday,
O lucky Father!

Come without warning
A friend of hurricanes,
Lightning in your bones!
We will open to you
The sun-door, the noble eye!

Open to rain, to somersaulting air,
To everything that swims,
To skies that wake,
Flare and applaud.

(It is too late, he flies the other way
Wrapping his honesty in rain.)

❖

Pardon all runners,
All speechless, alien winds,
All mad waters.

Pardon their impulses,
Their wild attitudes,
Their young flights, their reticence.

When a message has no clothes on
How can it be spoken?

—Thomas Merton

January

Merton awakened early on the first day of January feeling that something was walking around the hermitage, and by the time he had come fully awake, he realized it was raining.

His Mass in the novitiate chapel and the thanksgiving afterward were filled with reflection on the last thing he had read in the old year the night before—a letter of Peter Damian to two hermits, which recently had been republished by Dom Leclercq. The hermits wanted to be buried, when they died, at their hermitage and nowhere else. Merton agreed wholeheartedly with that.

In his mail that morning he received a letter from Webster College, which asked to have an exhibit of his drawings in April.

During the following week, Brother Joachim continued wiring the hermitage for electricity and Merton acquired an old two-burner hotplate on which eventually he could do his cooking.

The other major event was an exploration of about eight hundred acres of wild, almost unexplored land nearby called Edelin's Farm, which the abbot was interested in acquiring as a place to set up hermitages.

On Epiphany, January 3, Merton suffered what he called "a sort of emotional hangover" from his day in the woods on Edelin's Farm. He sat at the top of the field looking down on the hermitage and tried to meditate until he felt the return of calm. At dusk, he returned inside the hermitage, raked coals from the fire to one side of the fireplace and cooked his supper—"a thin potato soup made out of dust in an envelope."

Early January was peaceful for Merton. He catalogued his joys in the semi-hermit life. He found a little Nietzsche stimulating, but really preferred to read Isaac of Nineva in the hermitage or Zen masters out in the fields.

Each morning, when he went down to the abbey through the starlit woods, he either said Lauds or the Little Office of Our Lady, aware of the stars and light, the frost and cold, the ice and snow, the trees, earth, hills, and entering the lighted monastery among the sons of men.

The morning of January 17 was brilliant in the hours before dawn, with a deep snow and a sparkling moon. The fire kept the front room of the hermitage warm, and Merton looked forward to walking down to the novitiate in an hour. In the stillness, the weather was frigid. Whenever he stepped out on the porch, the bristles in his nose almost instantly froze, "and the outdoor jakes is a grievous shock."

On January 18, the British Dominican Father Illtud Evans arrived to preach the annual retreat. Sister Luke Tobin, of the Sisters of Loretto, came over with Father Illtud. She was on the sub-committee working on Schema 13[1] for the Vatican Council, one of the first women to be in such a position, and she wanted to discuss the work of the committee with Frs. Merton and Evans.

The annual monastic retreat was a particularly effective one for Merton, though he felt an element of emptiness and anguish from the concentration of it. But in the end, he was certain that he was obeying the Lord and was in the way willed for him, "though at the same time I am struck and appalled, more than ever, by the shoddiness, the slackness, the laziness of my response. I am just beginning to awaken and to realize how much more awakening is to come." Once again, he realized spiritually that he must renounce all ambition and self-seeking in his work and contacts. "I am so tied up in all this that I don't know where to start getting free."

Merton resolved to make his approaching fiftieth birthday the turning point, and simply "die" to the past, to live more abandoned to God's will and less concerned with projects.

The retreat ended January 26. It had been an important one for Merton, and he cherished his private talks with Father Evans.

The next day, the third Sunday after Epiphany, the monks at Gethsemani had their first concelebrated Mass.

On January 30, the eve of his birthday, Merton did his annual "summing up" without too much "agonia". Much of the speculation centered around the external events of his life. He awakened to a cold night, filled with the depth and silence of snow. He had cooked what he considered a far too elaborate supper the preceding night — soup, toast, sliced pear and banana; and he concluded that if there were no better reason for fasting, the mere fact of saving time would be a good enough reason. "For the bowl and the saucepan have to be washed, and I have only a bucket of rainwater for washing."

Taking only coffee for breakfast made more sense, because he could read quietly and sip his two mugs of coffee at leisure, and it was really enough for the morning.

He felt a greater need for discipline and meditation. The early morning hours were particularly good, though in the morning meditation of one hour he found he was easily distracted by the fire. An hour of meditation was not much, he conceded, but he could be more meditative during the following hour allotted to reading. His mornings were filled with his duties as novice master, which he did not find too taxing. That afternoon work had become a burden. Not only did he have to keep the hermitage clean and the wood chopped, but he had an enormous mail and an overwhelming writing schedule.

On the afternoon of the thirtieth, a bright, snowy afternoon with "delicate blue clouds of snow blowing down off the frozen trees," Merton forcibly restrained himself from too much work around the hermitage and made sure he got an hour's meditation, and promised himself to do more later. He mailed a revised version of "Rain and the Rhinoceros" to *Holiday*.

Later, in the evening, he continued his summing up. Should he look at the past and analyze it again? No, rather he would thank God for the present, not for himself in the present, but for the present that was God's and was in God. A quick review of the past indicated to the hermit a lack of love, or rather a selfishness and glibness with girls, springing from his deep shyness and need of love. But that was hardly worth thinking about now, twenty-five years later.

What he found most in his whole life was illusion: the need to be something of which he had formed a concept. "I hope I will get free of that now, because that is going to be the struggle." And yet he felt that he had to follow a "concept" of what he ought to be, to meet a certain demand for order and inner light and tranquility. But he must cease striving for these on his own. Rather he must remove those obstacles that prevented God from giving him these things.

"Snow, silence, the talking fire, the watch on the table. Sorrow."

But what was the use of going into all this? No, it was better to move about, to do things—wash his hands, which were dirty—say the psalms of his birthday:

> Yet you drew me out of the womb,
> you entrusted me to my mother's breasts;
> placed on your lap from my birth,
> from my mother's womb you have been my God.
> Do not stand aside: trouble is near,
> I have no one to help me!

Later that evening Merton added some notes to the effect that no matter what mistakes and illusions had marked his life, most of it had been happiness and some of it, at least, truth. The profoundest happiness had occurred in and around Gethsemani as well as times of terrible anguish. The best times, for the monk, had been the hours alone, either in the hermitage or in the novice master's room or simply out in the fields.

Before going to bed he realized momentarily what solitude really meant:

> When the ropes are cast off and the ship is no longer tied to land but *heads* out to sea without ties, without restraints. Not the sea of passion, on the contrary, the sea of purity and love that is without care. That loves God alone immediately and directly in Himself as the All (and the seeming Nothing that is all). The unutterable confusion of those who think that God is a mental object and that to love "God alone" is to exclude all other objects to concentrate on this one! Fatal. Yet that is why so many misunderstand the meaning of contemplation and solitude and condemn it.

On January 31, which again fell on the Fourth Sunday after Epiphany, Merton awakened long before daylight to a fiercely cold cabin. Though embers still glowed in the fireplace, it was below freezing inside. The monk lighted his Coleman lamp, built up the fire and began heating the water for his coffee. Sitting near the fire, with his feet on the hearth, he read: "When I go home I shall take my ease with Wisdom, for nothing is bitter in her company, when life is shared with her there is no pain, gladness only and joy (Wisdom 8:16)." Merton said that if he really knew how, he would set those words to a beautiful music. "I can imagine no greater cause for gratitude on my fiftieth birthday than that I wake up in a hermitage."

What more could he seek than this silence, this simplicity, this "living together with wisdom?" On that festive morning nothing else mattered, and he realized that he did not need to defend the solitary life, that he had nothing to justify. He needed only protect "this vast simple emptiness" from his own desires and illusions.

Through the cold and darkness, in the immense stillness, he heard the Angelus ringing at the monastery.

He brought his coffee and the honey he used for sweetening to his work table and reveled in the jeweled glistening of the honey in the lamplight, seeing it as a festival. With such birthday gifts as this, he saw more and more that he must desire nothing but to surrender his whole being without concern. The frozen woods were in this awareness, and also his trip up the hill the evening before at the time of a very cold sunset, and the loneliness; even the two small birds still pecking at crumbs he had thrown on the frozen porch.

When he went down to say Mass, he found all tracks covered by snow blown over the path except fresh tracks of the cat that hunted near the old sheep barn. "Solitude: being aware that you are one man in this snow where there has been no one but one cat."

February

On February 4, Father Louis received a "fantastic present from [Daisetz Teitaro] Suzuki"—a scroll with the Zen scholar's own calligraphy. The monk had never seen anything more impressive. "It will be wonderful in the hermitage—but no clue as to what the characters say."

About this time Father Merton was asked to prepare a paper on the hermit vocation for a meeting of canonists to be held at New Melleray Abbey in the spring. In preparation he reread a 1952 issue of *La Vie Spirituelle*, which was devoted to solitude. He was struck by the evident progress that had been made. In 1952 the tone of the articles was not hopeful, simply a statement of regret that the hermit life had practically ceased to exist. By 1965, the hermit life was once more a fact, and moving beyond the state where it was thought necessary for a monk to get exclaustrated in order to fulfill his monastic vocation to solitude.

Even as he worked on the first draft of the paper on eremitism, his own hermit vocation began to look more favorable. He had hints that he would be able to move to the hermitage full time soon. On February 11, it rained all day, and the monk did not get back to the hermitage until after supper.

At nightfall he sat at his work table in front of the window looking out to the porch, which shone with rain, and at low clouds being blown over the valley.

The rain turned into a furious storm—something Merton would ordinarily relish, but tonight he was troubled. He had received an invitation from Godfrey Dieckmann asking him to participate in an ecumenical meeting with Bernard Haring, Jean Leclercq, Barnabas Ahern and several others. The abbot had refused permission, again something that the monk would not ordinarily have given much thought. But this time he was filled with distress, for which he could not account.

"But I have to learn to accept this without resentment. Certainly not easy to do. So far have hardly tried and to tell the truth it angers and distracts me."

The distress persisted over the weekend. Father Abbot preached a sermon on vanity, ambition, using one's gifts for one's own glory. Merton could only infer that the sermon had something to do with his invitation to attend the meeting. The monk was depressed, and above all humiliated that he should feel it so much and be forced by his feeling to think about it all day. "How absurd. And yet the efforts I made to see it rationally as something trifling and laughable would not come off." Finally he lay awake half the night, something that had never happened before in the hermitage.

He wrote a note to the abbot, apologizing for having offended him and admitting that the abbot's sermon had made him miserable. He said that his writing and other work were not pure ambition and vanity, though there might be some vanity involved in them, and expressed the wish that the abbot would accept him realistically and not expect him to be something he could not be.

The abbot immediately sent back a note assuring Father Louis that his sermon had nothing to do with him, that he had no intention of hurting the monk and was most concerned. Father Louis dismissed it as an illusion on his part. "I was relieved that it was all settled. I am surely old enough to be beyond that."

On Monday, February 15, when Father Louis walked outside for a breath of air before his novice conference at the abbey, he saw men working on the hillside beyond the sheep barn. The electric line was being strung up to his hermitage. Throughout the day he watched them working on the holes, digging and blasting at the rock to set up the poles.

Galley proofs of the book *Gandhi on Non-Violence* arrived from New Directions. Father Louis sat out in the sun and corrected them immediately, finding the galleys contained few mistakes.

By Tuesday afternoon, the REA men had the electric poles in place and one man clung to the top of each pole, reminding the monk of a landscape of Stylites. "The light is coming. *Venit lumen tuum Jerusalem!*"

The monk hurried back to the hermitage in the early afternoon. Around 2:45, when Father Louis was translating some poems for Suzuki in return for his calligraphy, a foreman came and set up the electric meter. "I put on the switch and have light."

That evening Merton pronounced the light an unqualified blessing. He had thought he would dislike the two long fluorescent bulbs in the ceiling, but they were perfect for his needs and cast a stark, white light that fit in with his taste. They provided enough shadows in the corners and picked up the stones in the fireplace. Although he liked the icons much better in ordinary daylight or candlelight, the black ink on Suzuki's scroll was greatly improved by the new light.

The hermit celebrated the great event with a supper of potato soup, his first meal cooked on an old electric hotplate. He called it "an evening of Alleluia."

The dermatological problem with his hands began to worsen in the following week. The skin opened up and cracked, leaving deep holes that were painful. This condition interfered seriously with his work. Even tying shoes was painful and he had to wear gloves to make up his cot. On February 24 he walked down to the monastery to catch a ride in to see the dermatologist. While he was waiting for the ride, the brothers in the gatehouse made signs to him. "Good thing that fellow that wanted to kill you has gone away."

Merton deduced from the signs that some visitor in the gatehouse had become over-excited and decided to shoot him. The visitor had been disarmed and sent away by the monks. Also, in the morning's mail the monk received some hate letters regarding his writings on racism and on peace.

He rode in to see the doctor, who did not know what caused the dermatitis, but took skin samples for lab tests. He advised Father Louis to wear dermal gloves whenever he was working. Father stopped in Bardstown for supplies and was back in the hermitage in time to eat lunch.

That evening, with the rain pouring against his roof, the monk thought peacefully of death and accepted the fact that possibly some madman would find his way up to the hermitage and assassinate him. "And if that is the way it is to be I am glad to accept it from God's hands if He will give me the grace to die in a manner pleasing to Him."

He sat writing with dermal gloves. Everything about his hermitage filled him with joy. He saw it as the place God had provided after so much prayer and longing.

> I can imagine no other joy than to have such a place to be at peace in, to love silence, to think and write, to listen to the wind and all the voices of the wood, to struggle with a new anguish, which is nevertheless blessed and secure, to live in the shadow of the big cedar cross, to prepare for my death and my exodus to the heavenly country, to love my brothers and all people, and to pray for the whole world and for peace and good sense among men.

In this benign mood, Father Louis prepared supper and admitted that he now liked his own cooking: rice and pinto beans, with applesauce and some peanuts. "A nice meal!"

March

In early March, Father Louis continued his studies in preparation for his article on the hermit life. This led him to the realization that being a "part-time hermit" was simply not enough, and he prayed for the day when he could have genuine solitude on a sustained basis.

At this time, too, he began a serious study of the life and work of Simone Weil. Toward the end of Jacques Cabaud's book *Simone Weil: A Fellowship in Love*,[2] he discovered that his godfather and guardian, Dr. Tom Bennet, had treated her at the end of her life and had found her a most difficult patient because of her absolute refusal to eat. "Funny that we have this in common: we were both problems to this good man."

A period of good, calm work ensued. On Sunday, March 14, Merton went down to the abbey to shave and to give his regular afternoon conference, this one on Philoxenus, after which he remained to sing Vespers. He was particularly devoted to the Lenten hymns and dreaded the day when they would sing them no more.

It had rained most of the day, and turned cold. After Vespers the sky cleared. He walked up the hill and through the woods to his cabin as the sun was setting and with the moon already up. Inside he looked out the bedroom window and saw two deer grazing quietly in the field, in dim dusk and moonlight, hardly more than twenty yards from the cottage. Whenever he moved about, they would stop grazing, look up and extend their ears attentively. Eventually, he walked out on the porch and stood watching them until some signal sent them off "in a wonderful, silent, bounding flight down the field."

The peace was shattered in the next days as news of the events at Selma trickled in to him. For several days his attention was riveted to whatever he could learn about the gathering of people at Selma, and on the evening of March 18 he learned that Father John Coffield, who had been at Selma and was on his way back to Chicago, was at the guesthouse. Father Louis went down immediately to see the visitor. Father Coffield filled him in on the details, including the two murders that had taken place during the protest. Father Merton learned that the protest was national in scope, and articulate, and that congressional leaders were now determined to pass corrective legislation.

The following day, on the Feast of St. Joseph, Merton celebrated the twenty-first anniversary of his simple profession and the eighteenth of his solemn profession by concelebrating Mass for the first time.

In the afternoon he took some of the novices over to explore Edelin's knobs. Walking in very thick brush he was struck in the right eye by a sapling branch, wounding the cornea. The wound was painful but not serious. At the infirmary he was treated with ointments, an eye-patch was fitted, and he was also told to wear dark glasses.

That evening, unable to work, the monk sat at his desk near the fire and watched the light of a full moon on the pine trees.

For the next two days, he was unable to read well, so he spent most of the time gathering wood, preparing food and cleaning the cabin. He said the office, attempted to read with the left eye and wrote a letter to Nicanor Parra, the Chilean poet.

By March 23 the eye was better, though still not well, and Father Merton had the whole day at the hermitage. In the middle of the afternoon someone knocked at the door and the monk opened it to see Andy Boone, who owned the farm adjacent to the monastery property. In the conversation, Boone revealed that an excellent spring had got filled in some years ago about fifty yards behind the hermitage. They went through the thick brush to find it and Father Louis discovered a dozen places where deer had been sleeping. It delighted him to learn they were his nearest dormitory neighbors, that they slept not more than thirty or forty yards from his own bed.

They found the spring's location and the monk resolved to clear the place and perhaps pump it up to the hermitage as a water supply.

The weather turned too cold and rainy for any outside work, however, and Merton came down with a severe cold. He felt he caught it from being in the choir, where he got overheated, and then getting chilled going outside. On the morning of March 26 he supplemented his usual breakfast of coffee with a slice of rye bread, and read Ruysbroeck while eating, thinking of him in terms of Zen.

He spent the morning working in the novitiate, and his cold worsened. He felt he did much better in the hermitage, and left to return up the hill as early as possible. That afternoon Andy Boone came again, bringing the monk a check for some trees he had cut on the fence line.

April

In early April, Father Louis marked the trees Andy Boone was to cut down in the hollow behind the hermitage, where the spring was located. He remarked on the great tangle of brush, saplings, vines, fallen trees and honeysuckle that covered the area to be cleared. He had decided to use the spring for the hermitage and rhapsodized about the prospect of "a spring of sweet pure water."

Merton took great joy in the Masses of the week, especially some of the second tone melodies—the Introit, *Laetebur cor quaerentium dominum*, and he was deeply moved by the *Vexilla Regis* at Vespers. He wondered if these Gregorian masterworks would ever again be equaled. They reminded him of everything he loved about the world he had known as a child: the Romanesque churches, the landscape of Languedoc. "Useless to cling to all that, but I am humanly rooted in it."

As Holy Week approached, Father Louis concentrated on its solemnity and importance in his life. "I am a Christian, and a member of a Christian community. My brothers and I are to put aside everything else and recognize that we belong not to ourselves but to God in Christ. That we have vowed obedience that is intended to unite us to Christ, obedient unto death, even the death on the cross." He meditated on obedience. Insofar as they truly desired God's will in them, then even the smallest and most ordinary things were made holy and great, and their lives were transformed. He regretted that so much of monastic obedience had become formal and trivial, and felt that renewal must mean above all a recovery of the sense of obedience to God in all things, and not just "obedience to rules and superiors where demanded, and then after that go wool-gathering where you may."

One of the fruits of the solitary life was a sense of the absolute primacy of obeying God; that is, a sense of the need to obey and to seek His will, to choose freely to see and accept what came from Him, not as a last resort, but as one's daily bread. This led to a liberation from automatic obedience into the seriousness and gravity of free choice to submit.

On Palm Sunday, Father Louis gave his conference on Angela of Foligno and took supper at the abbey. Afterward, feeling exhausted, he returned to the hermitage and retired almost immediately. Within an hour he was awakened by the intestinal flu that was making the rounds at the monastery. He was sick all night, and remained nauseated and weak the next day, so ill he had to move into the infirmary where he got a good rest the following night and was able to take eggs for breakfast. He felt he had escaped easily and was well enough to return to the hermitage. Wednesday evening he feared he had returned too soon. Restless and feverish, he broke out in cold sweats, which required him to change shirts three or four times. He got up at three, made a poor meditation and fixed some Lapsang Souchong tea Jack Ford had given him. "It is the most effective medicine I have taken in all this — and it is marvelous tea."

The tea, with a slice of lemon and two pieces of rye toast, restored him remarkably. A heavy rain prevented him from going to the monastery for chapter and the *mandatum* of the poor. At dawn the rain lessened and the hermit looked out to the valley that was dark and beautifully wet. The redbuds were in flower and dogwood buds were beginning to swell.

He wrote in his notebook the phrase: "Obedient unto death."

This was his vocation as a monk — to live in simple direct contact with nature, primitively, quietly, "bearing witness to the value and goodness of simple things and ways and loving God in it all."

The moon was full on Saturday night when Father Louis walked down the forest path to attend the offices of Easter Vigil. He returned later under a moon so brilliant he could not see the stars. The woods were perfectly silent. He sat on the porch to make his thanksgiving after communion.

The monk awakened to the peace and beauty of Easter morning. At sunrise he walked out on the porch, looked about at the deep grasses and felt the soft winds on his face. The woods were turning green on the hills across the valley. He said the old office of Lauds accompanied by a woodthrush "singing the fourth tone mysteries in the deep ringing pine wood."

The early mornings of late April with the Easter moon in its last quarter high in the sky and the light of dawn spreading over the valley, filled the monk with contentment. He called it "the paradise season." In such hours he read Tertullian, *de Resurrectione*, finding the prose more powerful and captivating than any he had ever read.

On April 27, Father Louis received a copy of Jacques Maritain's notebooks, the *Carnet de Notes*, and began to read with care and a special personal interest, relishing particularly the photographs of Vera and Raïssa. "Though I never actually met them, I know they are two people who loved me, and whom I have loved through our writings and the warmth and closeness that has somehow bound me to Jacques and to them. It is really a kind of family affection. . . ."

May

When publisher James Laughlin came for a business visit on May 3, the two men went over the portion of the Chuang Tzu material that had been typed up. Laughlin was enthusiastic and Merton promised to "get at the rest of it."

He spent much of the rest of the month putting *The Way of Chuang Tzu* in publishable form. This work made him see again how far he was from the kind of hiddenness Chuang Tzu advocated. "Really, the problem is there: and wanting a 'hidden life' that is not after all hidden, but famous." Father Louis desired only the hidden life, but this desire, or the manner in which he sought it and lived it, had brought him the fame. He prayed that it would work itself out. "I am certainly getting sick of the contradiction."

Work on the Chuang Tzu book brought him a deeper peace. His inner climate harmonized remarkably with that of Chuang Tzu, and all the sights and sounds of those May days provided a perfect setting for this climate. "One lovely dawn after another. Such peace. Meditation with fireflies, mist in the valley, last quarter of the moon, distant owls—gradual inner awakening and centering in peace and harmony of love and gratitude."

In reply to a correspondent who thought all contemplation was a manifestation of narcissistic regression, Father Louis wrote that authentic contemplation was the contrary— a complete awakening of identity and of rapport. "It implies an awareness and acceptance of one's place in the whole, first the whole of creation, then the whole plan of redemption—to find oneself in the great mystery of fulfillment which is the mystery of Christ."

May 25 brought another full day at the hermitage. Father Louis came to see that only those days of total solitude were full and whole for him. The others seemed partly wasted, even when he appeared to have accomplished more. He worked for an hour in the morning, and another hour in the late afternoon on the Chuang Tzu book. In the afternoon he also worked outside, cutting back wild grape vines in the woods and burning brush piles.

Hot and tired from the physical exertion, he came back into the coolness of the cabin to prepare his supper. Jack Ford had brought him two loaves of pumpernickel bread from a Jewish delicatessen in Louisville a few days earlier, and also some Twining's Earl Grey tea. The monk served himself the pumpernickel, the tea and a can of mandarin oranges for supper. He ate in the front room at dusk while the birds continued to sing in the forest.

On Monday, May 28, still deeply transformed by his contact with Chuang Tzu the monk remarked on the "everchanging freshness of woods and valley. One has to be in the same place every day, watch the dawn from the same house, hear the same birds wake each morning, to realize how inexhaustibly rich and different is sameness." This was the blessing of stability, but it was not really evident until he experienced it alone in a hermitage. The common life distracted him from its fullness.

On Saturday, May 29, he finished the Chuang Tzu book. At dawn the following morning he went through the entire manuscript and was exhilarated by the effect of reading the work from beginning to end. He expressed gratitude to John Wu for insisting that he undertake this work. Now he had only to write the introduction.

The monk's stomach had not been the same since the intestinal flu. An appointment was made for him to go to Lexington for a complete check-up the following Friday.

In the refectory at the abbey, the reading was from Muriel Trevor's biography of Cardinal Newman, a work Merton followed with fascination. His admiration for Newman grew constantly as he learned more of the details of his life and "all the nonsense he had to suffer from almost everyone; and with what good sense and patience, after all."

On Monday, Dan Berrigan, Jim Douglass and Bob McDole came to discuss Schema 13 and the article on war. It appeared at that time that the article might contain at least some tacit approval of the bomb. Merton viewed this as an apocalyptic irony. "But we must do what we can to prevent a disgrace and scandal of such magnitude."

June

After their departure, he worked hard on the introduction to the Chuang Tzu book and finished it late in the afternoon on Thursday before he was to leave for Lexington and the medical tests on Friday.

The tests were almost unbearable to Father Louis. "When I began these examinations ten or fifteen years ago they were unpleasant but bearable. Since then my insides have become so sensitive that they are a real torment. However there is no cancer, there are no ulcers, just a great deal of inflammation and sensitivity."

Father Merton had to remain in the clinic over Saturday. He glanced through some copies of *Life,* seeing photos of helicopters in Vietnam, white mercenaries in the Congo, marines in Santo Domingo. This conglomerate produced for him one whole picture of an enormously equipped white civilization in combat with a sprawling colored and mestizo world armed with anything its inhabitants could lay their hands on.

> And the implicit assumption behind it all ... is that "we" are the injured ones, we are trying to keep peace and order, and "they" (abetted by Communist demons) are simply causing confusion and chaos, with no reasonable motives whatever. Hence "we," being attacked (God and justice are also attacked in us) have to defend ourselves, God, justice, etc. Dealing with these "inferior" people becomes a technical problem something like pest extermination. In a word, the psychology of the Alabama police becomes in fact the psychology of America as world policeman.

Father Louis returned to the hermitage Saturday evening, filled with relief to be back in the beauty and peace of nature, surrounded by the songs of birds. But the greatest joy of the solitary life did not come from the quiet, the peace it produced in the human heart, but in awakening and attuning the heart to the voice of God,

> to the inexplicable, quite definite inner certitude of one's call to obey Him, to hear him, to worship Him here, in silence and alone, and that this is the whole reason for one's existence, this makes one's existence fruitful and gives fruitfulness to all one's other acts, and is the ransom and purification of one's heart that has been dead in sin.

It was not simply a question of existing alone, but of doing, with joy and understanding, the "work of the cell," which was done in silence and not according to one's own choice or the pressure of necessity, but in obedience to God. "But the voice of God is not 'heard' at every moment, and part of the 'work of the cell' is attention so that one may not miss any sound of that voice."

The monk began to read, slowly and with great delight, Mai Mai Su's *Tao of Painting.* He remarked that she was becoming, along with Nora Chadwick and Eleanor Duckett, one of his secret loves. Nora Chadwick wrote him "charming letters" and Eleanor Duckett, an authority on monasticism, sent him a "beautiful spontaneous note written in the Cambridge Library on Ascension Day, with a splendid quote on the monastic life from a 9th century text."

On Friday evening, June 12, during a heavy rainstorm, Father Louis learned and sang the *Regnum Tuum Domine* from the Ambrosian Vesperale. This would serve, for a time, as a short dawn office along with the

Benedictus es and oration. He considered it one of the most beautiful chants he had ever found.

Final reports from his tests at the clinic revealed a staphylococcus infection in the monk's intestines and he was immediately put on antibiotics, which soon gave some relief.

On June 13, Father Louis went down to concelebrate Father Timothy Kelly's first Mass; on June 14 he concelebrated again with Father Barnabas Reardon. He considered them the best concelebrations they had had, with the concelebrants "really in it with their hearts. And I certainly was." On the bright calm Monday, Father Louis cleaned out the closet where he kept his typewriter and paper, and found an Ambrosian *Sanctus* that delighted him.

As one beautiful day followed another, Merton meditated on solitude and its implication for him, especially in light of the spirit of Chuang Tzu. Solitude was becoming less and less a "speciality," and he did not seek to "be a solitary" or anything else,

> for "being anything" is a distraction. It is enough to *be,* in an ordinary human mode, with one's hunger and sleep, one's cold and warmth, rising and going to bed. Putting on blankets and taking them off, making coffee and then drinking it. Defrosting the refrigerator, reading, meditating, working, praying. I live as my fathers have lived on this earth, until eventually I die. Amen. There is no need to make an assertion of my life, especially so about it as MINE, though it is doubtless not somebody else's. I must learn gradually to forget program and artifice. I know this at least in my mind and want it in my heart.

July

On July 2, Father Merton had another long day at the hermitage. The early hours were cool, and he read Bultmann and then decided to draft an open letter to the American bishops about Schema 13 and the chapter on war.

The morning's high point, however, centered around a non-meeting with his old and dear friend from the Louisville Carmel, Mother Angela Collins. She had written that she was going to Savannah to be the prioress in the Carmel there. The monk had replied that the southbound planes out of Louisville flew over the monastery properties and told her to be on the lookout. When the plane was due to appear, Father Merton walked out under the pines and waited. The jet appeared and flew over. "I suppose she saw the monastery and perhaps even picked out the hermitage, as I told her where to look." The monk watched the plane disappear, noting how moving this was for him, and how fond he was of Mother Angela. "She was one of the few people I could talk to absolutely freely about my ideas and hopes for the solitary life, which to a great extent she shares, and which she completely understands . . . I felt she was very much of a sister to me, and I am grateful for her."

Merton continued his speculations about solitude. He viewed it as highly dangerous if one did not work at it with complete honesty. Did his solitude meet the standards set by his approaching death? In a sense, the two went together in his mind. Solitude was not death, it was life; it aimed not at a living death but at a certain fullness of life.

> But a fullness that comes from honestly and authentically facing death and *accepting it without care,* that is with faith and trust in God. *Not* with any social justification: not with the reliance on an achievement that is approved or at least understood by others. Unfortunately, even in solitude, though I try not to and sometimes claim not to, I still depend too much emotionally on being accepted and approved.

He saw that his life and the witness of his solitude might have significance for the work, but felt that any justification in this order was a great danger to him. "It is one of the points where I see my defenselessness, my weakness, my capacity to pretend and to be untrue."

He could be true in his solitude in preparation for "the awful experience of facing it irrevocably in death, with no more hope in anything earthly, only in God (totally unseen)."

To do this without appealing to others for reassurance and approval was the goal toward which he must direct himself. How could others know, one way or the other? He observed that insofar as his journals were honest, they contained enough materials to destroy him in the eyes of small-minded men forever after his death. But that was the point: not to live as one who could be destroyed, or who feared disapproval. In order to be true, he must avoid ingeniously falling into ways of being "true" in the eyes of others and of posterity.

In July, Dom James indicated that he was working to make the change of novice masters, in which case Father Merton would finally be freed of all impediments to total solitude and could live the hermit life on a full-time basis.

The monk's one real difficulty with the faith at this time lay in accepting the Church as a redeemed community, not only juridically but so that in fact to follow the mind of the Church meant to be free from the mentality of "fallen society." Ideally he could see this, but in fact he found so much that was not redeemed in the thinking of those who represented the Church. That in Schema 13 the Church even risked officially approving the bomb was not a convincing demonstration of holiness and guidance by the Spirit in Merton's mind. "Naturally I must do much more praying and thinking about this question of the Church and see it more in depth than I do. Certainly I cannot accept a merely individualistic Christianity (authority for individuals, not for the Christian community). On the other hand, too external a view of the Church would be wrong."

The life of Newman, still being read in the refectory, was an inexhaustible source of clarification for the monk. "The reality is in his kind of obedience and his kind of refusal. Complete obedience to the Church and complete, albeit humble, refusal of the pride and chicanery of churchmen."

On Saturday, July 17, shortly after midnight, Father Louis was awakened by a violent thunderstorm, with continual lightning. One bolt of lightning struck the electric system and was grounded. "I felt the click of it through the whole house, and even felt as if electricity were coming out of my feet in bed."

The sense of peace that followed that early Sunday morning was deeper by contrast. Merton believed he could always know Sundays by a special atmosphere of peace and blessedness, even though all mornings were equally quiet and the same birds always sang. "This special peace is sensible, even where there are no signs of Sunday — such as the first Mass bell from the village church in New Haven, across the valley."

On Monday morning, July 19, long before dawn, Father Louis was up and working on his notes for the Schema 13 chapter on war. "The terrible thing is that a society that pretends to be Christian is in fact rejecting the word of God, and able to do so by the all-pervading suffocating noise of its own propaganda, able to make itself believe whatever it wants." What could one do? "It would be useless to pretend to be a prophet, for no one, as far as I can see, is 'sent' with any prophetic message. Least of all myself. Best I can do is the feeble attempt of the notes on Schema 13 to the *Commonweal*, Bishop Wright, Archbishop Flahiff and others."

Father Louis went down to talk with Father Abbot after chapter about his need for an appointment to see the proctologist soon, something he dreaded. "Painful, unpleasant business. I suppose this is part of being fifty." The abbot cheered him by confiding that on August 20, the Feast of St. Bernard, he would make the change in the novitiate and Father Louis would be free to live in the hermitage all the time with no further responsibilities except to give one conference a week in the novitiate on Sunday.

Merton was jubilant with the news, and chastened by it. "Things like this make me ashamed of my fears and worries and my suspicions of Dom James." He thought the abbot's decision was truly remarkable since this was a most unusual step in the order and one he could not possibly have taken two years before.

Concelebration after that conference was a moving and humbling experience for Father Louis who reproached himself for his resentments against the abbot and thanked God for enough light to see his own childishness in this.

That afternoon the monk walked in the quiet hollow behind the hermitage, thinking seriously about the change that was to come, which he viewed as "one of the greatest mercies of God in my whole life."

That evening he began a perpetual psalter, not to say a given quantity of psalms at any period of time, but just to keep the psalter going from then until his death. He needed the continuity the psalter offered, continuity with his own past and with the past of eremitism; and he decided it should be the Latin psalter. He viewed the psalter as a deep communion with the Lord and his saints. "To be in communion with the saints of my tradition is by that fact to be more authentically in communion with those of the Greek, Sinai and other traditions, which reach me through my own Fathers."

There followed days of great peace for the monk. He remarked that almost any day he could write "great peace" but this was a special and new dimension of peace — a tranquility that could not be attained by cultivation but was "given."

"One will, one command, one gift. A new creation of heavenly simplicity." However, this must be silent, secret, not for secrecy but because words would only falsify it.

An oppressive heat, the first of that summer, settled over the area. On July 24 the monk was too torpid to pray seriously, but he kept trying. He made orangeade for supper and put it in the freezer, thereby accidentally discovering how to make sherbet. He slept through the storms that came that night.

On July 27 he tried out the schedule he hoped to follow when he became a full-time hermit. He would go to the monastery only to say Mass and have his noon meal. He had considered going down for Mass after Prime, then going to the conventual Mass, returning to the hermitage and going back for the noon meal. But he saw this was not practical. He settled on the routine of going down late, around eleven, saying Mass at eleven-thirty, and returning after his meal.

This worked well. Not to run back and forth to the monastery was a relief, "and in the late afternoon, saying office before supper, I realized that a complete, total and solid peace had settled upon me — a happiness without afterthought and without reflection."

On July 28 he continued the same schedule, finding that with it he had time to taste the meaning of freedom: "And to taste, with all certainty, that free is what one is intended to be. For this one was created and redeemed."

He realized that men had a deep fear of authentic freedom. He himself had learned to fear it. He believed that without faith, living in solitude would be a different matter.

But with faith it becomes an eschatological gift. I have never before really seen what it means to live in the new creation and in the kingdom. Impossible to explain. If I tried I would be unfaithful to the grace of it — for I would be setting limits to it. It is *limitless*, without determination, without definition. It is what you make of it each day in response to the Holy Spirit.

The mood and spirit of such passages, and indeed of this solitude, are almost completely synthesized with his writings in *The Way of Chuang Tzu*. The monk felt that individuals could find such freedom in any setting, so long as they "unlearned" their fears, or removed the impediments to the kind of grace they were experiencing. Even his projected trip to St. Anthony's hospital did not produce its usual dread. "Who cares? It is God's will and His call. The same freedom is everywhere. It is not limited to places. Yet solitude, these pines, this mist, are the chosen locus of freedom in my own life."

August

Merton spent the first week of August in St. Anthony's hospital, under a strict medical and dietary regime and with nine hours of sleep each night. The hospital sisters surrounded him with thoughtfulness, bringing in magazines and even a box of candy. Though at the beginning, the monk called the hospital routines "a test of patience," by the end of the week he frankly relished the loving care and companionship of the sisters.

While Fr. Louis was in the hospital, Brother John of the Cross painted the hermitage to fill in all the cracks.

Merton was released from the hospital in greatly improved health on August 6, two weeks before "the big change." He returned to the silence of the monastery and hermitage with joyful anticipation, glad to be back in the simplicity of his life, glad to be freed from routines established by others.

To be on his own, to be human and to accept fully that he was human took on new meaning in the light of his preparations to live in solitude.

This fact that I am a man is a theological truth and mystery. God became man in Christ. In becoming what I am He united me to Himself and made me His epiphany, so that now I am meant to reveal Him, and my very existence as true man depends on this: that by my freedom I obey His light, thus enabling Him to reveal Himself in me. And the first to see this revelation is my own self. I am His mission to myself and through myself to all men.

How can I see Him or receive Him if I despise or fear what I am — man? How can I love what I am — man — if I hate man in others?

The mere fact of my manness should be an everlasting joy and delight. To take joy in that which I am made to be by my creator is to open my heart to restoration by my redeemer ... So pure is the joy of being man that those whose Christian understanding is weak may even take this to be the joy of being something other than man — an angel or something. But God did not become an angel, He became *man*.

By August 14, the Vigil of the Assumption, Father Louis had almost completed the frustrating task of cleaning out the novice master's office. The accumulation of books, notes, manuscript, letters and papers appalled him. Though much of it was material he had received unrequested, and set aside to read later, still he viewed the clutter as disgraceful. He promised himself never to forget this "awful, automatic, worried routine of piling up books, sorting papers, tearing some up, mailing them out and so forth," and hoped he would find the strength not to accumulate such materials in the hermitage.

"I wonder how many wastepaper baskets I have filled in the last week? And with this absurd ritual of waste paper has gone a rending of the intestines, diarrhea at night, *angst*. The revelation of futility and interminable self-contradiction. What a poor being I am."

Now that his departure into solitude was definite and near at hand, doubts assaulted Father Louis. But he was certain that he was in the right way and that to turn back would be an infidelity. In such moments of confusion, he recognized a hidden joy. Nor was it always hidden, since he experienced it openly and powerfully not only in the silence of the early morning "but also in the hot muggy afternoon which in these days is tropical."

His supreme affliction was to see his distrust of the Lord and his refusal simply to let himself go in hope. But to see that was also a joy, and he could begin to hope God would cure and transform him.

He was consoled in all of this by a letter he received from Naomi Burton Stone, a long-time friend and literary representative, in answer to one of his in which he admitted his own confusion and self-contradiction. He described her letter as "full of mature, realistic understanding, and feminine comfort—the warmth that cannot come from a man, and that is so essential."

He concluded that psychologically his doubt was based on the rift in his life, "the *refusal* of woman which is a fault in my chastity." But he was learning to accept this even if it meant admitting a certain loss. He saw chastity as his most radical poverty, and his lack of poverty in accumulating things

as a desperate and useless expedient to cover this irreparable loss which I have not fully accepted. I can learn to accept it in the spirit and in love and it will no longer be "irreparable." The cross repairs it and transforms it. The tragic chastity which suddenly realizes itself to be mere loss, and fear that death has won—that one is sterile, useless, hateful. I do not say this is my lot, but in my vow I can see this as an everpresent possibility. To make a vow is to be exposed to this possibility. It is the risk one must run in seeking the other possibility: the revelation of the Paraclete to the pure heart.

On the morning of August 18 the private council met and voted to approve Father Baldwin as the new novice master. Father Louis then retired and they voted favorably on his retirement to the hermitage – the first time such a decision had ever been taken in the long history of Gethsemani.

Long before dawn on August 20, the Feast of St. Bernard, Father Louis was up reading in Hebrews. After speaking of the faith and suffering of former saints, the writer concluded: "All these having borne witness to the faith, did not receive what was promised, because God foresaw something better for us, that apart from us they should not be made perfect" (11:40).

Entering his new life, the monk observed that he formed part of the promise and fulfillment for which others had suffered and hoped; in his turn he would suffer and prepare the way for others.

The day was festive in the community. Most were happy that Father Louis was going to live in the woods, "for the right reasons, I think – namely that it shows us opening up to the spirit, in awareness of new possibilities and not just the evasion that condemned everyone to uniform and rigid adherence to one set of practices for all, meaningful or not."

He received many notes from well-wishers on that last busy day, and in the afternoon he gave his final official conference as novice master. In this he explained his thoughts on the solitary life and concluded by asking for the prayers of the community:

> And when you pray for me, all I ask that you pray for is that above all I should completely forget my own will and completely surrender to the will of God, because ... this is all I want to do. I don't want to go up there and just sit and learn a new form of prayer or something like that; it is a question of total surrender to God. And I in my turn will pray for you to do the same thing ... The ambition of those Greek monks on Mt. Athos is that you get to the point where you are kissed by God.

In closing he described a picture of an Athonite hermit he had seen in some old text, a ragged old man with a crow sitting on his shoulder. The caption read, "He was kissed by God."[3]

After the conference, Father Louis took care of the last-minute details, and made arrangements about clothing. He asked to be given the old robes that had been discarded in community – not rags but robes that had been replaced four years before at Easter when new materials were brought into use. With the exception of his Sunday conferences, his daily Mass in the library, and a new manual for postulants the abbot requested him to write at the last moment, his official and set duties with the community were now over. He went into the woods, relieved of the burden of ambiguity that had created so much tension between his duties in community and his vocation to solitude. He went, as he said, not to find God in the silence and solitude, but because he believed that is where God wanted to find him. "I feel as if my whole being were an act of thankfulness."

By the next afternoon, after a good meditation and long study of Irenaeus, he reached Psalm 80 in the psalter and found that solitude gave a different horizon to the psalms, "precisely because one is alone with God and He speaks directly and personally, giving the light and nourishment one especially needs."

September

Hunters invaded the woods for the squirrel season. The monk was sure no squirrels could be left alive and he asked the men to leave. His mood was so benign, however, that "even this idiot ritual does not make me impatient. In their mad way they love the woods too: but I wish their way were less destructive."

Within the week, the reality of his solitude had brought its revelations and he felt deeply reassured that he was in the right way for his vocation. Even his stomach problems had cleared up.

A week after he had asked the hunters to leave, "a beautiful, bushy-tailed red squirrel appeared on the porch and darted about before leaving. It was a delight to see him. How can they kill such beautiful, live things?"

Gradually the dispersion and agitation of his pre-solitary days faded into a quiet, productive tempo as natural energies replaced nervous energies. In this kind of solitude, he experienced everything as equally blessed.

The blessing of Prime under the tall trees, in the cool of early morning behind the hermitage. The blessing of sawing wood, cutting grass, cleaning house, washing dishes. The blessing of a quiet, alert, concentrated, fully "present" meditation. The blessing of God's presence and guidance . . . I am very aware of the meaning of faith and fidelity, and of the implications of the relationship they establish. This place is marked with the blessed sign of my covenant with Him who has redeemed me. May I never fail this goodness, this mercy.

Despite his trips down to the monastery, his solitude was virtually uninterrupted. Each morning at 10:45 he went to say Mass, do his necessary errands, have dinner and return up the hill with his gallon jug of drinking water. The community respected his solitude, and most days he spoke to no one.

So, I am beginning to feel the lightness, the strangeness, the desertedness of being really alone. It was far different when the ties had not been cut and when the hermitage was only part of my life. Now that everything is here, the work of loneliness really begins, and I feel it. I glory in it, giving thanks to God; and I fear it. This is not something lightly to be chosen and unless I were convinced God had chosen it for me I could not stay in it.

By the third week, the real loneliness was setting in. When the monk went down to say his Mass, he saw most of the community out gathering the potato harvest under a late summer sky, and he recalled the communal beauty of work, the sense of brotherhood and joy when he had been able to participate in cutting tobacco or husking corn.

For a moment, watching them at work, he felt an overwhelming sense of loneliness. After supper he walked outside the gate of the hermitage enclosure, said some psalms and meditated looking out over the bottoms and across at the distant knobs. Everything came alive and he realized that he must not fall into the trap of taking himself and the hermitage too seriously, of tying himself to that little cottage as if his whole life was bound up with it. He became aware that the house was not important, and most of all the "hermit image" must not become a matter of role playing. "My first obligation is to be myself and follow God's grace and not allow myself to become the captive of some idiot idea, whether of the hermit life or anything else. What matters is not spirituality, not religion, not perfection, not success or failure at this or that, but simply God, and freedom in His spirit."

He did not even like the idea that the hermitage was "his." Since he was a homeless body, being tied to a home disturbed him. He would move toward viewing the place as any other hole in the wall that was not his. In this, he felt that fasting would be important. He would cut down on all that "cooking of rice and canned vegetables"—though he still had some rice and cream of wheat, which he would not scruple to use in cold weather.

"Meanwhile I am impatient of all desires. May the Holy Spirit bring me to *true* freedom."

The moon became full on the night of September 10. When the hermit stepped out on his porch at moonrise, he saw a doe in the field. She had become accustomed to him, and he could walk about saying Compline without disturbing her. In fact, she came down the field toward him.

This disturbed him, because soon the hunters would be out to hunt the deer. He hoped the doe's growing tameness was confined to that one association, with the white hermitage and the monk in black and white.

After Compline, he returned inside to bed.

By September 11, the monk's mail showed that rumors were flying to the effect that he had "left the monastery." Although he had notified his friends of the move, stating that visits and mail would be vastly curtailed in the future, and most had viewed this as a great blessing for his vocation, the truth was scrambled in the rumors. In a sense this amused Father Louis. "The general reproach is that I am not clinging, in spite of reason, grace and everything else, to something God no longer wills for me—clinging to it just because society expects me to do so!"

If this provided scandal, it was salutory scandal and he viewed it as proof of the reality of his vocation. "Hence I see my task is to get rid of the last vestiges of pharisaical division between the sacred and sense, between the sacred and secular, and to see that the *whole* world is reconciled to God in Christ; not just the monastery, not only the convents, the churches, and the good Catholic schools."

The monk began to focus his afternoon work on preparation of the book *Conjectures of a Guilty Bystander*—a rewriting and rearrangement out of sequence of his journal notes from the preceding years. The journal notes served only the skeleton, however, since he rewrote a great deal. "For instance, rewrote an experience of March 18, 1958, in light of a very good meditation of Saturday afternoon, developed and charged . . . in a word, transforming a journal into 'meditations' or '*pensées.*'"

On September 25, Father Louis had a visit from Father Chrysogonus Waddell and Father Flavian Burns. Father Chrysogonus had just returned from Europe, where he had visited many of the scenes of Merton's childhood. He brought a booklet on St. Antonin and some postcards of Montaubin. At St. Antonin, Father Chrysogonus had met Madame Fonsagrives, the wife of the doctor who had cared for the youthful Tom Merton. She told Father Chrysogonus that her husband had discovered TB in the youngster. Father Chrysogonus was astonished, but when he brought the news to Father Louis it elicited no reaction, so Father Chrysogonus did not know if Father Louis had ever known or suspected the exact nature of his childhood illness.[4]

After the two visitors left, Father Louis leafed through the book about St. Antonin, which had been sent by Madame Fonsagrives. He had no recollection of Dr. Fonsagrives. He had not known before, however, that Dr. Fonsagrives had diagnosed his condition as TB. "That is why I had to go to Murat and also why I had special food in the infirmary at the *lycée*. I was never told."

As September ended, the hermit was well, despite the fact that his hands had broken out again. He kept busy splitting and gathering up the firewood for the winter, preparing *Conjectures* and deepening his life of prayer.

On the evening of the thirtieth rain blew out of the dark valley. Wind bent the tall pines and Father Louis anticipated the storm would last all night. "I have been walking up and down on the porch for an hour and am full of the joy of it. Somehow I seem happiest when rain encloses my solitude."

October

In October, the long days without companionship began to appear in all its starkness to the monk. He had no regrets, but he saw that he needed a "common life . . . I need the saints and angels with me in my loneliness." He developed an authentic sense of companionship in the woods and cabin with his choice of friends—Jacques and Raïssa Maritain and Vera Oumonçof—in one imaginary gathering with him; Boehme and Rilke in another. By mid-October he was getting closer to Rilke, someone he had met in passing for years "but never really talked with."

He began a serious and prolonged study of Rilke, reading the poems aloud, then singing them, improvising melodies.

Brother Dunstan finished typing the manuscript for *Conjectures of a Guilty Bystander* on October 19, and Father Louis found the manuscript much bulkier than he had expected.

During the next two days he had visits from Ernesto Cardenal, who spoke with him about the new experimental community Cardenal was founding on an island in Lake Nicaragua; and from Hildegarde Goss-Mayr, a courageous peacemaker, who was in this country on a lecture tour. Merton's profound admiration for both visitors, and his intense interest in their work, made him feel that the intrusions were necessary and fruitful.

They were gone again by the evening of October 23, which also marked a turning point in the weather. The heavy rains had broken and the weather turned cold. Father Louis noted that his woodchuck had buried itself completely, covering the entrance to its hole, and had gone to sleep for the winter on its bed of leaves. "I wish him a happy sleep! And today is very autumn-like—cold clouds flying, trees half bare, with leaves lying around everywhere, the broad valley beautiful and lonely. The wonderful mysterious lovely sense of an autumn evening. It is not the autumn of Rilke's poems, something more hard, solid, yet more mysterious."

Merton began to experience the dangerous power of solitude working in him. It was easy to err in such an uncharted life, and the errors could go on undetected. He sensed the need to work at overcoming his weakness and tepidity, but caught himself again and again simply throwing himself into hard work as though that in itself were an antidote. At the end of October he came to the conclusion that all the meaning of solitude could be lost by following the habits one had brought out of the common life. "One has to start over and receive, in meekness, a new awareness of work, time, prayer, oneself. A new tempo—it has to be in one's very system (and is not in mine. I run.)"

He found that he needed to use the early morning hours for more silence and peace. But being quiet was not enough. He put his breakfast later and made his morning meditation longer.

November

On November 2, Father Louis wrote his friend and publisher, James Laughlin, to accept an offer of books. He feared that one of the errors into which he could easily fall in solitude was the development of bad or stale writing habits.

Yes, I would be glad to get something to read from New Directions. What do you think would help me to write better? Especially to keep the vocabulary from getting stale or me from getting into ruts, mannerisms, etc.? I used to like very much Lorca and Dylan Thomas — but remember our life here obligates us to steer clear of even what is merely indifference to the interior life. In other words — it is not that we are forced to lock ourselves up with a pile of pious trash, on some purely *a priori* basis. But what we read should help us to know God either directly, in Himself, or through knowledge of people as He has made them — or by contrast as they have made themselves. Anyone who has anything to say about the ultimate meaning of life or of the world is therefore o.k. But if it is just good experimental writing for its own sake, I guess perhaps not. If this sounds unintelligible, it would perhaps be more sensible to give you the rule in its ordinary formulation: No newspapers, no magazines, no radios, no movies, no books on stamp collecting, no fashionable novels, no textbooks on astronomy. But I notice a lot of the brothers with books on agriculture, so anything corresponding, in the field of the craft God has given me to follow . . . Verse would be at least tolerated. Anyway, thanks, and do send your catalogues. Maybe I will receive them, maybe not.[5]

Having completed *Conjectures,* Father Louis began gathering and editing the materials for the book *Raids on the Unspeakable.* As always, he did much rewriting.

On Thursday morning, November 11, Father Louis received a special delivery letter from Jim Douglass, in which he learned that on the previous Monday a member of the Catholic Peace Fellowship, Roger Laporte, had burned himself to death in front of the United Nations building in protest against the war in Vietnam. Even though the Catholic Peace Fellowship, of which Thomas Merton was a sponsor, lamented Roger Laporte's desperate act and was in no way implicated in it, the monk did not know this.

Shattered by the tragedy, he realized the impossibility of his position in being deprived of current information and yet making statements or having people take actions under his apparent sponsorship that were repellent to him.

He immediately requested permission from the abbot to send two telegrams. The first was to Dorothy Day:

JUST HEARD OF THE TRAGIC DEATH OF ROGER LAPORTE. AM DEEPLY SHOCKED AND CONCERNED ABOUT DEVELOPMENTS IN PEACE MOVEMENT. WILL THESE DO GREAT HARM TO CAUSE OF PEACE. DO THEY REPRESENT A RIGHT UNDERSTANDING OF NON-VIOLENCE. I THINK NOT. THOMAS MERTON.

The second was to Jim Forest of the Catholic Peace Fellowship:

JUST HEARD ABOUT SUICIDE OF ROGER LAPORTE.
WHILE I DO NOT HOLD CATHOLIC PEACE FELLOWSHIP
RESPONSIBLE FOR THE TRAGEDY CURRENT DEVELOP-
MENTS IN PEACE MOVEMENT MAKE IT IMPOSSIBLE FOR
ME TO CONTINUE AS SPONSOR FOR THE FELLOWSHIP.
PLEASE REMOVE MY NAME FROM LIST OF SPONSORS.
LETTER FOLLOWS.

That morning Father Louis also learned from Dan Walsh that a newspaper man in Louisville was trying to contact him. He supposed it had
something to do with Laporte's suicide, about which he knew practically
nothing. "Sometimes I wish it were possible simply to be the kind of hermit
who is so cut off he knows *nothing* that goes on, but that is not right either."

The next few days were desolating for Father Louis. Almost immediately
he began to wonder if he had not been too precipitate in sending the
telegram to Jim Forest, if he had not in fact committed an injustice. He
spent the next day fasting, chopping wood and praying.

On the morning of November 13, when Father Louis was saying Prime
under the pine trees in front of the hermitage, he saw a wounded deer
limping along in the field, one leg incapacitated. Added to his grief over
the sickness and violence of the world, the sight broke him and he began
to weep uncontrollably.

"And something quite extraordinary happened. I will never forget standing there weeping and looking at the deer and the deer standing still looking
at me questioningly for a long time — a minute or so. The deer bounded off
without any sign of trouble."

On November 20, Father Louis began to prepare answers to letters he
had received from Dan Berrigan, Jim Forest and Dorothy Day. He was
now convinced that their trials, especially the death of Roger Laporte, had
been handled with "much purity of love."

Now, he felt he had to clarify his own position, since people were iden-
tifying him with all the activities of the peace movement, most of which he
knew nothing about, such as draft-card burning. This showed him once
again a certain incompatibility between his solitary life and active involvement in any movement.

The letter that most preoccupied him was a lengthy rebuke from John
Heidbrink of the Fellowship of Reconciliation, obviously written in heat
and frustration after Father Merton's telegram to Jim Forest. In this letter,
John Heidbrink maintained that the dedicated life of those working actively
in the world was vastly superior to Merton's life in a hermitage "quilted in
mist."

Having portrayed my worthless evasion as hermit, he then dangles
before me the man I "might become" if, turning from this utter waste,

I would marshall all I have led into the cloister and lead them back into the world, back into his world of Bonhoefferish-Robinsonian concern, in which I would be welcomed and appointed a scoutmaster.

He speaks of being a "man for others" (the Robinson term). His letter evidently manifests what this means to him. To be "for" me means for him to mind my business without understanding it, to propose to me his own fantasies, and get me to harmonize with his own rhetoric.

In his response to Heidbrink, Merton apologized for any harm he might have done the peace movement with his telegram. He explained that he often heard about events, from disturbed people, after the events occurred, and was expected to make statements about them when he did not even know they had happened.

For instance, at the moment, while a lot of people think I am solidly behind draft-card burning, others are urging me to come out against it, while for my part, recognizing that I am not really in a position to make a really serious judgment, I would prefer to say nothing. You may regard this as cowardice, I do not. I don't think that Christian courage demands that one speak his mind regardless of whether or not it makes real sense. For the same reason, I gave up signing manifestos for ads in the newspapers on this and that issue.[6]

December

In a subsequent letter to Heidbrink, dated December 4, Father Louis enlarged on these points. He consented to reverse his decision and leave his name on the list of sponsors for the Catholic Peace Fellowship, but with the clear understanding that although he was morally and spiritually united to their goals, when it came to political and practical decisions,

I remain independent and autonomous and ... your acts are not necessarily my acts in this realm. I think in all fairness I need this clear autonomy for the sake of this free functioning my present life demands. I can be of use to you, I hope, if I don't have you hanging around my neck like what seems to me (rightfully or wrongly) a millstone. I do not say this position is a wonderful one, or deny that it may be simply the reflection of a certain incapacity on my part, a definite limitation. All I ask is that if it is a limitation you agree willingly to accept it patiently and not harass me for it, with enough confidence in me to hope that I will work my way through the woods in good season.

The monk agreed that an immoral war demanded political protest, but he reserved the right to make his own protest in his own name whenever he saw fit, and he did not want his name associated with forms of protest on which he had not been consulted in advance.

Although Father Louis regretted having sent the telegram of resignation, which had now been rectified, he considered it a "salutary" mistake in that it had led him to re-evaluate his position.

"I see how much there was that was inauthentic in my own initial enthusiasm for identification with peace activists . . . It was in reality selfish and naive at the same time: and I did not foresee that necessarily they and I could hardly go along forever in agreement, living in totally different circumstances."

In one area, he had no doubts. "I certainly want to support their professed aims — education, information, help of COs, etc., but not necessarily their bids for publicity and political action."

In the midst of the trials and distractions connected with his involvement in the peace movement, Father Louis realized dimly that something else was breaking through into his awareness. All of this activity was important, all of it had its place, but for him it would be fatal to become involved as if it meant that he gave it a place of primary importance.

What he called "a great event, a new presence" arrived: a Byzantine icon from Salonika, from around 1700.

The most beautiful I have ever seen (except in photos, of course). The Holy Mother and Child and then on panels that open out, St. Nicholas and St. George, St. Demetrius and St. Chorlandros — whoever that is. It was sent as a gift by Marco Pallis and I was moved, *bouleversé* by its arrival. How magnificent it is in its simplicity. I never tire of gazing at it. It will change my whole attitude.

The emotion he felt over the new icon helped him establish what was primary in his life: God's self-revelation to the monk in Christ and the monk's response in faith. "In the concrete, this means, for me, my present life in solitude, acceptance of its true perspectives and demands, and the work of slow reorientation that goes on. Each day, a little, I realize that my old life is breaking loose and will eventually fall off, in pieces, gradually. What then?"

His solitude was not, like Rilke's, ordered to a poetic explosion. Nor was it a mere deepening of religious consciousness.

What has been so far only a theological conception, or an image, has to be sought and loved. "Union with God." So mysterious that in the end man would perhaps do anything to evade it, once he realizes it means the *end* of his own ego-self-realization, once for all. Am I ready? Of course not. Yet the course of my life is set in this direction.

With the approach of Christmas and the end of the year, Father Louis worked quietly on preparing *Raids on the Unspeakable* for publication and giving his attention to solitude.

On December 21, while he was saying Mass, he heard the bells ring for an agony and guessed they were for Brother Gerard. An hour or so later, Father Amandas made him a sign that Brother Gerard had just expired.

A portion of Merton's Advent meditations centered on death as he tried to make some sense of his own eventual end. In the mail that day, he found a letter from a distant relative, in which was enclosed an old snapshot taken when the relative and his wife visited Douglaston thirty years before. The monk studied the photograph of himself as a vigorous young rugby player from Cambridge and was astonished to realize that was a totally different body from the one he had now, "one young and healthy, one that did not know sickness, weakness, anguish, tension, fatigue, a body totally assured of itself and without care, perfectly relaxed, ready for enjoyment."

And now the change. The monk said he would not mind such a change if he were wiser, but he was not so sure he was. He felt those were better times; the world had not yet heard of Auschwitz and the Bomb, even though all of that had already begun.

He compared his body then with the kind of body he bore now, with its arthritic hip; its case of chronic dermatitis which obliged him to wear dermal gloves much of the time; its sinusitis, chronic since his arrival in Kentucky; its lungs with scars from past illness; its perpetual diarrhea; its loss of hair; its loss of most of its teeth; its degenerating vertebrae, which caused his hands to go numb and his shoulder to ache, and for which he sometimes needed traction. With all of this, he had few moments when he was not aware that he had something wrong and that he had to be careful. "What an existence! But I have grown used to it—something which thirty years ago would have been simply incredible."

On Christmas Eve, Father Louis set his alarm and got up to go to the abbey for Midnight Mass. He walked through the dark woods in rain and high winds, jubilant with the excitement of the weather. He thanked God he did not feel the depression that had attacked him at Christmas occasionally in the past. He believed this came from his new thinking about death, which had opened out during the last days of Advent, when he had come to see death as built into his life, and accepting it in and with life rather than trying to push it out of life. "Death is flowering in my life as a part and fulfillment of it."

The rain had stopped when he returned through the darkness to the welcoming silence of his cabin. He made his thanksgiving quietly at Lauds, had a bite of food and went back to bed for a couple of hours.

He awakened to Christmas Day, said Prime and read for a while. It was the kind of day he liked, especially for Christmas—dark, cloudy, windy and cold, with a light rain blowing from time to time; a day not too bad for walking out on the wooded hills, "cold and lonelier than ever and full of apparent meaning. They talk to me of my vocation."

1966

The Night of Destiny*

In my ending is my meaning
Says the season.

No clock:
Only the heart's blood
Only the word.

O lamp
Weak friend
In the knowing night!

O tongue of flame
Under the heart
Speak softly:
For love is black
Says the season.

The red and sable letters
On the solemn page
Fill the small circle of seeing.

Long dark —
And the weak life
Of oil.

Who holds the homeless light secure
In the deep heart's room?

Midnight!
Kissed with flame!

See! See!
My love is darkness!

Only in the Void
Are all ways one:

---

*"The Night of Destiny" celebrates the end of the Muslim fast, Ramadan, and commemorates
the giving of the Koran to Mohammed. Hence it has something of the Spirit of Christmas, a
feast when the heavens open and the "Word" is heard on earth.

Only in the night
Are all the lost
Found.

In my ending is my meaning.

—Thomas Merton

January

Heavy rains pounded the roof of the hermitage, deepening the hermit's sense of solitude. He viewed it as a good beginning for the new year. In lulls between storms he walked outside and looked across the valley to "black wet hills sharply outlined against the clouds, and white patches of water everywhere in the bottoms." It was the kind of stark landscape he loved.

In his cabin, seated at his work table with the fire at his back, he opened a new ledger notebook to begin his journal notes.

Once again he had received an invitation from Ernesto Cardenal to join him in his newly-founded community at Solentiname in Nicaragua. Merton viewed this as perhaps an authentic expression of the will of God and left himself open to the possibility that he might be sent. However, with his back in such poor condition and his almost chronic intestinal problems, such a venture now appeared hazardous to him. On January 3, the monk made this invitation the intention for his Mass, said Mass attentively and asked nothing but the grace to do God's will.

On January 16, Merton received Rilke's *The Sonnets of Orpheus* in German with an English translation. He set himself the task of translating it straight through "without fearing to write nonsense." He hoped this would help him to stop holding back from the German and believed he knew enough German and was sufficiently attuned to Rilke to be right in some first guesses. He would then check his translation against the official ones.

The annual retreat was to be preached by Bishop Fulton J. Sheen. Merton, who liked Sheen, had permission not to attend the conferences but to visit with Sheen privately.

On the evening of the retreat's beginning, the monk stayed up late because that happened also to be the "Night of Destiny" *(27* Ramadan), which he viewed somewhat as a Moslem equivalent of Christmas: heaven opens to earth, the angels and the Spirit come down, all the prayers of the faithful are answered.

"Night of joy and peace," Merton wrote. "I shared the joy of the Moslems and prayed for them and for my own needs and for peace."

Winter's first snow fell. The next morning, January 19, the monk saw small deer tracks when he went down to say Mass at the abbey. Dan Walsh gave him a drip coffee maker he had picked up at an auction for $1.25. After Mass, Merton carried the coffee pot, his mail and his drinking water up the iced hill. He used the pot immediately for his breakfast coffee and noted it was the best he had tasted in a long time.

As the snow increased, he abandoned his plan to cut wood in the afternoon, but he did manage to haul a good supply he had already cut into the woodshed to dry out in case the storm continued.

In the dim blue light of afternoon, with the temperature dropping toward fifteen degrees, Merton worked on Nishida, Rilke and Octavio Paz. He enjoyed the Paz especially and decided to "overcome a certain laziness with Spanish writers" by not sticking with the obvious and easy works when he should tackle difficult ones like César Vallejo's last book of poems evoking the reality of the Spanish Civil War, *España, Aparta de Mí Este Cáliz.*

The snow continued heavy for two days, a blessing to the hermit for it helped guarantee his solitude. No one would attempt to approach the hermitage in such weather. The illusion of time, of clocks and hours, dropped away. This freedom, with its accumulation of silence and solitude, elevated all aspects of his existence to the level of felicity. All activities fused in the miracle and he could no longer make any distinction between what are called the lower and the higher elements of human living. His work, study, prayer and meditation flowed into acts needed to sustain his hermit life in the forest: to keep the fire going in the hearth; to sweep bits of straw and kindling used to start that fire; to pour a glass of drinking water and warm it by the fireplace for brushing his teeth; to put stale bread crumbs on the porch and then watch the gathering of cardinals, mockingbirds, titmice, myrtle warblers and the small white-footed mice with their brown fur and big ears that scurried from the woodpile; to break ice in the rain barrel so the birds could drink, and draw from it a bucket of water to wash his coffee pot and dishes; to retrieve from the bareness of his kitchen shelf the large mason jar he used for his "night vessel" when the weather was too cold to go outside, and place it on the cement floor under his cot. In that climate of interior freedom each act was filled with joy and thanksgiving.

On the afternoon of January 22, Father Louis stuck splinters in his hand hauling in logs for the fire. He walked through the deep snow to the monastery infirmary to have them removed. Picking up his supplies and mail, he hurried back to the forest, regretting even the intrusion of mail into his solitude. His frustration grew when he tried to answer a query from one of his publishers about quotations from Auden and Eberhart he had not properly footnoted. He could not find them. As a result he did not say Terce and Sext until mid-afternoon. Another search for the references was fruitless. By late afternoon he was tired and distracted, but praying the psalms, drinking hot tea and listening to the silence of snow gradually reordered everything for him.

On January 23, Sunday, the hermit awakened long before dawn, stirred the embers into a full fire and quickly made a pot of coffee, which he thought was better than anything he had tasted in years.

At his work table, in the circle of light from his crookneck desk lamp, he "suddenly wrote a French poem." This lengthy work, beginning with the line, *"Je vous lis les sonnets d'un capitaine aveugle,"* was later published in French as section 35 in *Cables to the Ace.*[1]

With a satisfaction that had come from having done good concentrated work, Merton dressed to go down to concelebrate Mass in the abbey. He set out in the deep snow, stopping to study fresh deer tracks which told him that two deer had jumped the fence in front of the hermitage. He regretted that he had not seen them, but with his desk light in front of him, he could not see out the window when it was dark. Since the snow had not yet obliterated them, he knew they were recent.

The monk was deeply chilled by the time he reached the abbey, and concelebrating in the heat of the building, he was soon soaked in sweat. With flu making the rounds of the community, Merton wondered if he should continue to concelebrate in weather like this.

The Introit for the Third Sunday after Epiphany was the same as that chanted the day of his birth almost fifty-one years earlier: *Adorate Deum, omnes Angeli ejus* (Psalm 96:7-8), and although it was now chanted in English as "Adore God, all you his angels" Merton thought of it as Latin, the language in which he read the psalms. The sense of that Introit followed him back to his cabin where he reflected on the role of prayer for the hermit. To be snowed in was to be reminded that this was a place apart, "from which praise goes up to God and . . . my honor and responsibility are that praise." That was his only joy, his only importance. "For it *is* important. To be chosen for this."

Merton's spiritual reading was in Second Corinthians. He continued his thanksgiving, remarking that the Spirit had made it possible for the veil to be removed from his heart. "It would be so easy to remain with one's heart veiled (as Rilke did in some sense) and it is not by any wisdom of my own, but by God's gift that it is unveiled."

The monk spent much of the rest of the day reading Nishida's *The Unity of Opposites* and making notes from it, remarking, "Nishida is certainly the one philosopher to whom I respond the most."

Monday, January 24, was the coldest day of the year, down to five below zero. The skies remained dark. The monk spent most of the workday writing a first draft of his preface to Ernesto Cardenal's meditations *La Vida en El Amor,* which Merton admired. Some had been written when Cardenal was a novice at Gethsemani. Merton wrote that although Cardenal left because of ill health, it was not the only reason; it did not make sense for him to continue as a novice and student when he was already a teacher.

A feature article about Merton was run in the Sunday Magazine section of the Louisville *Courier-Journal.* Although he had cooperated with the newspaper, the idea of any article about him was depressing. He imagined that everyone in Kentucky had seen the piece, except the monks. Dan Walsh could be counted on to bring a copy. "I don't anticipate being thrilled, only embarrassed and wearied."

On the eve of his fifty-first birthday, the monk learned that newspapers all over the country had picked up the story from the *Courier-Journal.* He hoped it would be considered his way of saying good-bye "and getting out (of public life) for keeps." His profound involvement with the works of Chuang Tzu and other Tao and Zen masters over the past years made any public notice appear to be almost a betrayal of his true vocation. His renderings of Chuang Tzu, published only the year before, were fresh in his consciousness. "The man of spirit . . . hates to see people gather around him," wrote the Chinese master. And "Achievement is the beginning of failure. Fame is the beginning of disgrace." Now similar aphorisms were Merton's own convictions, convictions derived from his own solitude and contemplation. Merton resolved that the one central option for him lay in letting go of all that might suggest getting somewhere, being someone, having a name and a voice, following a policy and directing people in "his" ways. What mattered was to love and to be in one piece in silence and not to try to be anybody outwardly.

This "summing up" occurred during a day of splendid snow, and it was brought on by the approach of his birthday. He found it ironic that he should arrive at the determination not to have any public identity at the very moment when newspapers were carrying the story about him.

"Life is very funny! *Vive la niege!*"

He decided that in the future he would write a lot of letters saying no.

His physical condition would help him to refuse. His back was getting worse; his hands were cracked and in such bad shape that he could hardly type at all.

On his birthday, January 31, the temperature fell to ten below zero. Merton celebrated with a couple of "fine walks," staying on his own hillside. He expressed astonishment and gratitude that he should be so old. Enclosed by the snow the cabin was particularly peaceful and so was the monk, who finished reading the sermons of Isaac of Stella.

February

The cold snowy weather continued into February. The monk remained at peace, doing good work. On the third, when his own typewriter was almost beyond use, Brother Benedict presented him a new Hermes, which delighted him. Merton typed with enormous rapidity using only the index and third fingers of each hand. He was deeply involved in those quiet, cold, snowbound weeks in researching and translating the Desert Fathers and preparing an article on spiritual direction in the Desert Fathers.

"I don't know what happens to *time* in this hermitage," he wrote on February 7, Feast of St. Romauld. "Three and four hours in the predawn go by like half an hour. Reading, meditation, a few notes, some coffee and toast — there is not much to show for it, but it is probably the most fruitful part of the day."

February 17 was threatening and bitterly cold. From the open door of his outhouse, Merton watched a woodchuck open up its den and come out after three months of hibernation. Merton thought the animal had "gone crazy" to come out in such weather. But the day proved the woodchuck right. The morning grew brilliant and the change spread its contagion to the hermit. He felt the hint of spring as only someone living close to the cold could. This was the mission of humankind, he exclaimed. "The earth cannot *feel* all this." He remarked that living away from the earth and the trees people fail them. "We are absent from the wedding feast."

Merton reflected on the moments of great loneliness he knew in his solitude but these were followed by other deeper moments of hope and understanding, as this morning, which would not be possible in their purity anywhere but in solitude.

After lunch, when he returned to the hermitage from his walk, the whole hillside was so bright and new that the monk wanted to "cry out," and he wept from the emotion.

"With the new comes also memory: as if that which was once so fresh in the past (days of discovery when I was nineteen or twenty) were very close again, and as if one were beginning to live again from the beginning: one must experience spring like that. A whole new chance. A complete renewal."

Within the week, on Ash Wednesday, the "curse" was on the skin of the monk's hands again and his back was so much worse it was decided he must go into Louisville for a medical examination. An appointment was made for March 3.

March

As always, a deep repugnance filled him as time for the examinations approached. On March 2, he simply took refuge from intellectual activity in physical occupations, feeling that to work silently in the woods was a more important and significant means to understanding than a lot of analysis and writing on the things of the spirit.

The next morning, Merton walked through a warm grey dawn to the abbey, where he took a hot bath in the infirmary and got into secular clothes to go into Louisville.

The x-rays showed that a back operation was unavoidable, and surgery was scheduled for March 24, with Father Louis to enter the hospital on March 23. He returned to the hermitage and sat up late, listening to a heavy rain pour against his roof and letting the idea of the surgery sink in.

From the time of the decision until his entry into the hospital, the monk took his deepest consolation from manual labor. He began the work of cleaning up around the hermitage, to leave the grounds in relatively good shape since he surmised he would be unable to do such work for a while after the back operation. The weather turned cold again, and on Saturday evening, March 5, the hermit burned brush and watched flurries of snow fall into the flames.

The next morning, he walked in the woods and studied the patterns in the water of his favorite hidden creek. He attempted to arrange his thoughts about life and death, "and how impossible it is really to grasp the fact that one must die. And what to do to be ready for it? When it comes to setting my house in order I seem to have no ideas at all."

In the evening he stood on the porch and studied a small herd of five deer through field glasses as they passed the brush piles beyond his fence less than a hundred yards from his cabin, entranced by their perfection.

On Tuesday, March 8, after a cold night, the sun warmed the morning. Father Louis thinned out young trees in the woods to the north of the hermitage — "enjoyable work while I can still swing a brush hook." In the afternoon Brother Benedict brought two walnut trees, which the two monks planted in the field in a small grove of pecan trees. Merton felt this was proper for a hermitage, though he himself could not eat them because of his intestinal problems. He hoped some other hermit in future years would make good use of the walnuts and pecans.

As the date for surgery approached, Merton had great difficulty in adjusting to the idea. But he could see that the condition of his back was such that if it were not done he would hardly be able to work with his hands and arms. His hand became numb after holding a pen and writing only a few lines.

He did manage to finish up the first draft of an article entitled "Apologies to an Unbeliever," which he planned to send to *Harpers'* before entering the hospital. He had many doubts and hesitations about this article but was pushed to write it out of compassion for Victor Hammer, "who is, after all, a very believing 'unbeliever' and for others who have to be alone and confused, penalized for the sincerity which prohibits facile options."

The weather turned springlike. On March 21, the Feast of St. Benedict, Father Louis began to prepare to go to the hospital. He lighted warm fires in the predawn hours, even though the temperature was down only to forty-five, in order to clear the woodpile from the porch. He boiled three eggs for supper, to use up the eggs, and because it was a feast day. He prepared his coffee with honey to consume the honey and because he was no longer using sugar as sweetener. And he read Angela of Foligno, whose "intense purity, sincerity, penance" reminded him of the warm clear light of the Florentine primitive painters.

In the darkness before dawn on March 23 Thomas Merton listened as the bell tolled slowly for the preface of conventual Mass at the abbey. Wind swayed the heavy pines in the night.

He turned off the icebox and took out a small package of oleo to return to the infirmary kitchen when he went down.

He remarked that if he could be serious, he was so now. He did not feel alarmed or concerned. "Yet I know I have to die sometime and may this not all be the beginning of it?"

If so, he accepted it in full freedom and gladness. He offered his life with that of Christ, and if the end were now, he would go that way gladly. He felt gratified too that the operation would coincide with the big protest against the Vietnam war and noted that it was his way of being involved.

The bell rang for the consecration at the monastery.

His sometimes negative feelings about the community were gone.

Certainly the spirit of the community is excellent and the place is blessed. There are very good men here. It is a sincere and excellent community. Fr. Chrysogonus is writing fine new melodies which are very authentic, probably as good as any church music being written now. In fact, may turn out to be the best. This is an extraordinary man. Father Flavian may soon be a hermit, and he has impressed many with the seriousness of his life of prayer. Fr. Eudes is doing an excellent job. Father Callistus is a good prior. And so on. Dom James himself has done immense good to this community by stubbornly holding everything together. He, too, is an extraordinary man, many sided, baffling, often irritating, a man of enormous will, but who honestly and in his own way really seeks to be an instrument of God. And in the end, that is what he has turned out to be. I am grateful to have been part of all this.

Merton remarked that his hermit life had been the greatest gift, and that he was just beginning to get grounded in solitude. He felt that if his life were really on its way to ending, his one regret would be the loss of years of solitude that might still have been possible.

After saying Mass at 9:30, he left in the car driven by Bernard Fox. It rained heavily during the drive into Louisville and Merton was glad because it lessened the danger of fires in the woods.

Surgery was delayed until March 25, the Annunciation. On that Friday morning he was taken to the operating room. He was aware of a woman, introducing herself as the anesthetist, Dr. St. Pierre. Dr. Thomas M. Marshall, the surgeon, was wearing a green suit.

An anterior cervical fusion was performed to correct the cervical spondylosis, using a graft from the left ilium.

Merton recovered consciousness in his room and asked what time it was. He was told it was 11:00 P.M., which surprised him for he had imagined that a day had gone by and he had missed communion. He was also astonished to find he could lie on his back without pain.

The first week was difficult, Merton recalled, but on the whole he had less trouble than he anticipated. "The worst was just the strain of the abnormal mechanized, routinized life of the hospital, poked and pushed and stuck and cut and fed and stuffed with pills, juices etc."

❖

With the World in My Blood Stream

I lie on my hospital bed
Water runs inside the walls
And the musical machinery
All around overhead
Plays upon my metal system
My invented back bone
Lends to the universal tone
A flat impersonal song
All the planes in my mind
Sing to my worried blood
To my jet streams
I swim in the world's genius
The spring's plasm
I wonder who the hell I am.

The world's machinery
Expands in the walls
Of the hot musical building
Made in maybe twenty-four
And my lost childhood remains
One of the city's living cells
Thanks to this city
I am still living
But whose life lies here
And whose invented music sings?
All the freights in the night
Swing my dark technical bed
All around overhead
And wake the questions in my blood
My jet streams fly far above
But my low gash is no good
Here below earth and bone
Bleeding in a numbered bed
Though all my veins run
With Christ and with the stars' plasm.

Ancestors and Indians
Zen Masters and Saints
Parade in the incredible hotel

And dark-eyed Negro mercy bends
And uncertain fibres of the will
Toward recovery and home.
What recovery and what Home?
I have no more sweet home
I doubt the bed here and the road there
and WKLO I most abhor
My head is rotten with the town's song.

Here below stars and light
And the Chicago plane
Slides up the rainy straits of night
While in my maze I walk and sweat
Wandering in the low bone system
Or searching the impossible ceiling
For the question and the meaning
Till the machine rolls in again
I grow hungry for invented air
And for all the compromising answers
All the gambles and blue rhythms
Of individual despair.

So the world's logic runs
Up and down the doubting walls
While the frights and the planes
Swing my sleep out the window
All around, overhead

In doubt and technical heat
In oxygen and jet streams
In the world's enormous space
And in man's enormous want
Until the want itself is gone
Nameless bloodless and alone
The Cross comes and Eckhart's scandal
The Holy Supper and the precise wrong
And the accurate little spark
In emptiness in the jet stream
Only the spark can understand
All that burns flies upward
Where the rainy jets have gone
A sign of needs and possible homes
An invented back bone
A dull song of oxygen
A lost spark in Eckhart's Castle.

World's plasm and world's cell
I bleed myself awake and well

Only the spark is now true
Dancing in the empty room
All around overhead
While the frail body of Christ
Sweats in a technical bed
I am Christ's lost cell
His childhood and desert age
His descent into hell.
Love without need and without name
  Bleeds in the empty problem
  And the spark without identity
  Circles the empty ceiling.
     —Thomas Merton

As the monk began to improve, he remained outwardly a good and cooperative patient, but privately he began to devise means of avoiding the constant medical attention he received from the nurses. Most of all, he loathed the bed baths and the hot compresses applied to his hip twice a day. Attempts to evade or postpone them were completely unsuccessful, so Merton brought his sedated powers of concentration into focus and plunged into a study of Eckhart.

Wednesday morning, March 30, found Merton lying on his back in pain, reading Eckhart, dreading the morning interruptions. The door opened. A young student nurse entered. Merton had not seen her before. Instead of silently inserting a thermometer and taking his blood pressure and writing on a chart, she spoke. Human communication took place. She introduced herself as Margie Smith and made a little speech to the effect that she had been assigned to take care of him, to handle the compresses and give him his baths and keep his room clean. The monk groaned inwardly. Here was a talker. Here was a beautiful young lady who was going to talk. He would not get back to Eckhart that morning. When she left for supplies, she made another speech at the door, telling him it was an honor to care for him. That meant she knew who he was. Even the anonymity he craved was to be denied. She would be handling not just another middle-aged patient with a room number, but Thomas Merton and whatever individual image she might have made of him.

Merton waited, cataloguing his reactions. Usually he was happy to be left alone. Now an astonishing sense of regret seized him and he wondered when she would be back.

She returned to apply the hot compresses to his hip, to make up his room, to give him his bath and a back rub. They talked easily. She had been in a convent. Her father was an artist who loved nature and solitude. What did Merton think of the new liturgy?

April

From that first encounter, Merton, who had before sought to avoid attention, now devised pretexts to have Miss Smith return, and prolonged the visits as much as possible. She also invented pretexts, bringing him extra sandwiches or reading materials whenever she had a free moment.

They talked hungrily and incessantly. Merton lent her his manuscript preface to the Japanese edition of *Thoughts in Solitude* in an effort to help her understand his hermit vocation. He believed her to be a solitary who fought solitude, feared it and rejected it. They had run into each other as questions. He hoped his preface might help her by providing some answers. Too, they were united in one painful common aspect of their experience: a loss of illusions about the character of religious organizations at the level of power manipulation and pure human ambition.

"We have seen too much of the dark side of that moon, the side that is not illuminated by the sun of Christ," wrote Merton in his preface, which disturbed the young student nurse. She needed other people, she insisted. It was inconceivable that Merton professed not to. Merton explained that she had misunderstood. His vocation was not a rejection of humanity. On the contrary, his vocation was to a solitude centered in God that ultimately united him to all humankind. From these conversations emerged the tacit admission of need for a profound friendship with one another at the spiritual level.

By Friday, though it was painful, Merton was able to go for a short walk. He found this a great help. But he felt that Margie Smith's affection, now open and undisguised, was the greatest help in restoring him to life. He realized that although he was generally indifferent to the society of men, at least in the sense that he could live without being lonely for his fellow monks or other male friends, he did feel a deep emotional need for feminine companionship and affection, "and seeing that I must irrevocably live without it ended up tearing me up more than the operation itself."

On Saturday morning, April 2, she did not come. Other nurses did her work in the monk's room and he felt consumed with loneliness. He learned that she was ill.

The pain in his back worsened that afternoon, particularly when he sat up. Determined to say Mass the next day, Palm Sunday, he refused to give in to the pain, sat up and copied pages from Eckhart. By evening, the pain was so severe he feared he would never make it through Mass.

The next morning, Margie Smith was still indisposed. Merton perceived that his life had begun to be different in that when she was present he felt "light, free of care, a sense of deliverance, a feeling that things were as they ought to be — one might almost say a sense of being 'saved.'"

After an extremely difficult Mass, Merton returned to his room and rested for a while. In the afternoon, he went down for a walk behind the grotto. He walked slowly, alone, saying the office, moved by Jeremias, but lonely and hurting and cold. He noticed a building he took to be the nurse's dormitory and wondered which might be the window to her room. He remained longer than he should have in the hope that she might see him and come down "and I would somehow change my direction and be there to meet you as you came by the grotto, and it would be as though we had met by accident."

She returned to her duties on Monday. "The room was filled with the light of freedom and joy," Merton wrote. "Pure joy. So pure one never even thought of it as 'joy.' But when someone else came in, you knew that the false worlds of roles and hospitals and social artifices had once more intruded into the world of pure play and pure joy, the world of laughter that was completely without care. We did not know, of course, that we were now in love."

Merton noted that they were transparently happy people set apart from the rest of the human race by this charmed happiness that did not look beyond the moment or beyond the confines of the hospital.

On Tuesday morning in Holy Week, Merton had the strength to read the entire Passion during the Mass. Returning to his room he was overjoyed to see Margie in the hall in front of the cafeteria. They talked for a moment. Merton waited in his room. She was delayed, and Merton attempted to read Eckhart. But he was unable to concentrate and noted that his thoughts of Margie had defeated Eckhart completely.

Finally, Margie Smith came and began her work of bath, compresses, making up the room. Her instructor looked into the room to ask what was keeping her so long. After they had left, the instructor told Margie Smith that Merton's love for solitude was serious, and that she should not spend so much time making up his bed and caring for him.

Tuesday was her last day to care for the patient. Wednesday was her day off, and she was leaving for a trip to Chicago. She promised to come tell him good-bye.

Wednesday in the early afternoon, Merton went for another walk behind the grotto. He had confirmed that the building he had seen before was the dormitory where she lived. In fact, she had seen him from her window the previous Saturday. He hoped she would see him now, because he needed to go across the street to the drugstore and wanted her to accompany him. When she did not come, he made his way to the drugstore and bought a box of ear plugs because he was having difficulty sleeping at night.

Late that afternoon, she came to his room and he saw her for the first time out of uniform. For the first time he stopped calling her Miss Smith and used her first name.

> We were in a different relationship. You were Margie. I see the back of my notebook on which you wrote your name and address before leaving. It is here beside me, a kind of presence of you. You were now the person I would think about in long sleepless nights (beginning this very rainy night). The person whose name I would try to use as magic to break the grip of awful loneliness on my heart.

They did not find much to say to each other. She asked if she could visit him at the abbey. The monk told her the truth, that it would be difficult to get permission to see her. Both were ill at ease. He realized she interpreted his reply as meaning that he was no longer interested in her.

Finally, though Merton wanted her to stay, he told her she must not be late for her plane. They said good-bye and he thanked her. She took his hand between both of hers and held it a moment then hurried out the door.

Merton returned to his bed and allowed the desolation of her absence to fill him. He listened above the drumming of rain for her plane and thought he heard it flying low into the clouds over the hospital.

When, after hours of wakefulness, he finally drifted into sleep, he dreamed they were together in a city "where we could not find our way to the center that was 'real.' "

At the Holy Thursday Mass, Merton concelebrated, "sweating, determined, grim, with my back hurting. It was just a question of getting through." At the end, however, he thought he had begun to see clearly a truth about their relationship. "In a sudden flash of unity, I saw it all beyond desire and beyond preoccupation." Their attachment for one another simply was a presence in God. "Thus, I do not need to have a project of forgetting her or of remembering her—or any other special 'yes' or 'no.' There is nothing special I have to *do*—just to move on in freedom and without care."

Though on Thursday the monk had reduced the question to this comfortingly detached intuition, on Good Friday the human reality of his situation struck him when he found himself sweating under compresses that had not been put on by her. Suddenly he felt his whole being in revolt against the prospect of not seeing her again.

The monk admitted that he was in love with her and now, having admitted it, he must find some way of coping with it. There was no question about the primacy of his vocation and vows. To seek an obvious human fulfillment of that love was also out of the question. No, it would have to be a matter of their being present and active in each other's lives in a profound spiritual friendship, which Merton summed up in the word "devotion."

What disturbed a man of his honesty was the already passionate nature of this devotion. He tried to argue that he was not seeking happiness with her as opposed to his choice of seeking happiness in God alone. For the moment, this opposition seemed curiously confused. But it was not merely the question of his vow of chastity. It went far deeper, to the very roots of his being. "To seek happiness in human love now would be as absurd as a fish getting out on the beach to walk ... My chastity is not merely the renunciation of sin or of sexual fulfillment but the renunciation of a whole mode of being, a whole conception of life and of myself."

At this point he dismissed his desire for her, his longing to see her again and even his project of commitment and devotion as something akin to "hallucinations."

But the idea of devotion returned. The next day when he left the hospital, he left her a note telling her how she might write him and indicating that he hoped the friendship would continue.

Father Louis returned to the abbey where he was to be lodged in the infirmary during his recuperation. He arrived in time to say the Easter offices. His memory returned to the hospital and to his reading and copying sentences from the sermons of Eckhart. He hurried to the hermitage "silly with exaltation" to be back where he belonged. There "everything else drained off and Eckhart remained as real. The rest was like something I had imagined."

The activity caused a mild relapse. During the night in the heated infirmary, Merton sweated profusely and had to change clothes three times. He felt completely disoriented and longed to be in the hermitage during the rain.

On Easter morning he forced himself up and made his way to the hermitage, where he spent the day "in a kind of daze."

By Tuesday, April 12, the hermit had resumed his regular hour's meditation "and began to get myself together again."

Merton's physical condition improved steadily, particularly the hip incision. He began to sleep with less nocturnal sweating. He was becoming more himself but was astonished at the effort it took to return to normalcy "after some great trauma has broken in on you."

On April 19, ten days after the monk's return to the monastery, warm winds swayed the fully-leafed branches of the hedgeroses at the hermitage. The fragrance of the first grass cutting filled the air and dogwood blossoms had begun to show in the forest. Brother Benedict finished planting the pecan trees, and a letter arrived from Margie Smith.

The letter contained four sheets of paper, two with pictures of Peanuts characters, one with Linus and his security blanket, another with the dog lying on top of his doghouse saying "It's good to have a friend." Her letter, though not a love letter, was of a kind to awaken love and tenderness in the monk. She identified her loneliness with his solitude, saying that although he did not necessarily feel loneliness in his solitude, perhaps at times he did, and when he did he should always remember that he was being thought of often with much love and fond friendship. She accepted with sadness the realization that she would never see him again.

"Have to think my way around the problem of this tenderness," Merton wrote, "but anyway I will do the only thing possible and risk loving with Christ's love, where there is so obvious a need for it. And not fear."

But he was determined it must be a Christ love, "the love of a man dedicated to God — a selfless, detached, free, completely open love."

She had given him a way out by accepting the fact that they would not see one another again. Quickly, before he could consider the wisdom of that, Merton wrote her a frank and simple statement that he loved her and knew she loved him, and that surely they would meet again.

His letter frightened her. It did not agree with the image she had made of him as a remote and ideal person, a perfect and untouchable figure full of calm wisdom and inexhaustible sympathetic understanding. She wanted him to be ideal, someone she could love with a deep devotion, "almost a cult." Merton felt compelled to destroy this cult projection because he simply could not live with it himself. At the same time his letter expressed desire. "She feared a desire that would consume the cult object she had set up for herself."

Merton had reproached himself about his youthful relationships with women because he had always been selfish, taking what he could and then running when the attachment risked getting serious. For twenty-five years in the monastery he had simply, as he remarked, side-stepped the whole question of human love, and he was now moved to face it squarely. He believed that if he could remain sufficiently unselfish, he could risk loving Margie Smith in a way that would not conflict with his solitary life, his life devoted to God, but would simply enrich and deepen his vocation.

He entered into a long series of speculations and justifications, which he later viewed with dismay as not much more than rationalizations permitting him to pursue his longing with some degree of good conscience. It was deeply necessary, critical even, at this point in his life to prove to himself that he was capable of a purely unselfish love. Otherwise he would go on being haunted by the fear that he might be like certain Christians described by Léon Bloy, who were incapable of loving anyone or anything and therefore persuaded themselves that they loved God.

"Who knows anything at all about solitude if he has not been in love, and *in love in his solitude?* Love and solitude must test each other in the man who means to live alone: they must become one and the same thing in him, or he will only be half a person." The monk's journals and notebooks of this period are filled with speculation of this nature, which he might easily have rebutted or at least qualified. But with his long training in searching for and accepting reality, his almost brutal honesty and his "writer's" ability to function as an objective observer of even his own subjective holocaust, Merton decided in this experience to leave things as he wrote them. He was too intelligent not to perceive the importance of his quandary, and no matter how it turned out, no matter how it made him look, he wanted the truth of its essentials to exist in an unembellished state in his notes.

Certain other factors made Merton believe the attachment might be providential. His surgery was changed from early to late March. If it had occurred as first scheduled, he would not have met Margie Smith. At fifty-one years of age, and after twenty-five years of monastic experience in an essentially masculine society, he was highly susceptible to the charms he found in the companionship of women. The hospital experience itself, the medical destruction of certain reserves of physical modesty through sedation for pain and through the necessarily intimate handling of his body by nurses left him with a high vulnerability to the idea of a love that could be profound and yet not impugn his vows or his vocation. Persuaded that this attachment was from God, he trusted God to protect the love and keep it from damaging either of them.

The next few days were peaceful. He had salvaged the relationship he could not bear to terminate, and that was enough for the moment. All attention now was given to his spiritual life and to the work that needed to be done.

On Friday night, after having dinner with a visiting abbot and having drunk some wine served with the dinner, Merton suddenly decided to try telephoning Margie's residence. He dialed on the direct line to Louisville and reached Lourdes Hall only to learn that she was out for the evening and was not expected back before midnight. Merton went to bed shattered and bitter with himself, not only because of the disappointment in not reaching her, but also because his attempt had involved an illegal phone call, one for which he had not sought or received permission. Merton loathed this kind of surreptitious irregularity in himself or anyone else in monastic life, and viewed it as little more than "sneaking."

Yet the next morning he was out looking for a phone again. He could not get into the gatehouse. He wandered to the cellarer's office and discovered the phone there also had a direct line to Louisville. He called again, but made a mistake. He returned at noon and attempted another call, finally tracing her to the cafeteria. Her cry of joy when she recognized his voice banished his doubts. He told her he would have to come in to the doctor on Tuesday, and they agreed to meet. They spoke of their love, emphasizing that it had to be pure and in keeping with his vows, a chaste love.

"I have loved you like that from the beginning," she said.

Nevertheless, she was frightened enough to consult with a priest, without mentioning Merton's name. The priest told her that she must never see him again, send no message, give no explanation, not see him at all.

Merton had his own fears. The compulsion to make those phone calls showed him how little he could trust in his self-control. It sickened him to have to act illegally and in such a calculating way. He had excused himself in the guise of charity, wishing only to help her. Now he admitted that he could do her little good as long as he was so emotionally attached. He must try to be free and more sure of what he actually meant by love in Christ and careful not to delude himself.

Sunday, the Second Sunday after Easter, a ravishing spring day brought him no relief. He suffered the torments of conscience for having wasted so many hours the day before in his vain attempts to reach Margie. He was losing weight, five more pounds that week, and he felt a strong repugnance for food.

The call, yes, it had been necessary, and it had cleared some of the confusion between them.

"Yet, on the other hand, one thing leads to another, and this is another link in an uncomfortable kind of karmic chain." Now they were committed to another meeting. He reproached himself for not having followed his original intention and been content with a few letters and nothing more.

"Sooner or later it will all end anyway, and it would be better to end it before it gets more complicated than it is."

That afternoon, Merton resumed his regular Sunday conferences at the abbey for any of the monks who cared to attend. He read one of his hospital poems to the conferees, and was gratified not only by their reaction to the work, but by their apparent joy to have the conferences and Father Louis back.

In the infirmary that evening, exhausted and troubled, the monk felt sure he would be unable to sleep. Brother Camillus Epp, the infirmarian, persuaded him to take a sleeping pill. The infirmarian also found an old bottle of bourbon stored in a closet since the days when Dom Edmund Obrecht was abbot. He administered a medicinal dose and Merton slept nine hours, awaking only to change his sweated clothes.

The rest restored him. His somber intentions and guilts of the twenty-fourth were altered the morning of the twenty-fifth. Now he was certain his response of love to Margie was right. "It might have nothing to do with the rule books or with any other system, it might be open to all kinds of delusions and error, but in fact, so far, by and large, I have been acting right."

Tuesday, a grey, rainy morning, Merton went into Louisville for a check-up. He met Dr. Wygal, on whom he depended for transportation around Louisville, and told him about Margie. Dr. Wygal openly and frankly disapproved. After his check-up, the two men waited in the hall of the Medical Arts building. Margie appeared from around the corner wearing a white rain coat, "small, shy, almost defiant with her long black hair and grey eyes."

Introductions were made. All of them were uncomfortable as they went to lunch at Cunninghams. Dr. Wygal left them for a half-hour to take care of some errands. Alone, they began to relax. Merton read her the poem he had written in the hospital and sensed her change, "as if her whole being opened up to me again and warmth came radiating out from her at all the right moments in the poem." Fear vanished. They could talk. They talked precisely about their fears. She was certain the monk did not understand what he was getting into. "I might make you love me in a way that would harm you," she said. Merton told her he understood that but he had another viewpoint. He did not want passion, only a deep, abiding, affectionate relationship. They could love one another without being erotic. Sex, he explained, was simply a sign of a deeper union. Since they already had that deeper union, they did not need the sign of it. What mattered was simply the union of their hearts. Consumed by erotic attraction they nevertheless agreed that purely spiritual love was their goal, "and the rest can be controlled."

After the two men had dropped Margie off at the hospital, they discussed the attachment and Merton's ideas about it on the way back to the abbey. The doctor had grave doubts, feared the monk was deluding himself, and told him so in terms Merton noted as "his warnings, prophecies of doom and gloomy insinuations."

That evening Merton examined his situation again and admitted that he was now "in deep" but resolved to fight for this "sweet, tender good friendship" against all odds because "I *do* believe in this kind of love." He compared it to the relationship between Raïssa and Jacques Maritain and remarked that he had known something of this already in pure friendships with certain nuns with the difference that Margie was "so terribly inflammable and beautiful."

Perhaps the most terrible anguish in Merton's adult life had begun. His thoughts were obsessively connected with Margie. Each phone call increased the need for further communication. "I respond so much to her now, to the inflections of her voice, her laughter, everything, that I was flooded with peace and happiness and wanted just to talk to her forever."

They exchanged long letters professing their love and their aspiration to the highest kind of love—letters filled with the very passion they were determined not to unleash. The monk turned to poetry again—the poems written for or about Margie. He sent them to her or read them to her over the phone.

At the end of April Merton began consciously resisting the temptation to make more phone calls, attempting to break through his obsession and find ways back into prayer.

"There is *no other way* but deep prayer, renunciation of all surreptitious desires for self-satisfaction and consolation and a firm determination to love her only in God."

Solitude in the hermitage for at least part of the day was his greatest help. After a few hours there he was "at peace and relatively sane again."

May

May began with pouring, continuous rain. On the second, Merton put on his raincoat and went for a walk: "The desolate yet beautifully rain-soaked fields were a joy." In the emptiness, with no cars and no people—"just larks rising out of the green barley or whatever it is"—he found peace. He was not lonely for Margie but felt she had somehow become part of his solitude and part of his life that "tries to be in God, tries to dwell at the point where life and grace well up out of the unknown."

The experience gave him the clue for which he had been groping: this was the only way their love could become a harmonious part of his vocation. Never during this crisis did the monk doubt the primacy of his vocation or the essential tragedy of any departure from that vocation. The problem lay in finding the means to transform a passionate, physically-tormenting love into one sublime enough and generous enough to salvage both of them and at the same time harmonize with his vocation as monk and hermit. If they could manage this, it would be fruitful, "but it also presupposes the Cross. Always!"

On May 4, Merton received permission to invite the Jack Ford family and friends out to the abbey for a picnic on Derby Day, the following Saturday. He also got permission to make the necessary phone calls. He asked the Fords to bring Miss Smith. Then he made a legal call to Margie.

"She has settled down to a sweet little-girl happiness that completely disarms and ravishes me," he wrote after the call. "I just don't know what to do with my life, finding myself so much loved and loving so much, when according to all standards it is all wrong, absurd, insane."

On the following day, Thursday, Merton's close friend and publisher, James Laughlin, arrived to discuss publishing projects. He was accompanied by the Chilean poet Nicanor Parra, whose work Merton greatly admired.

The next afternoon the three men decided to take a drive through the radiant spring countryside. They went to Bernheim Forest where Merton hoped to find a public telephone. Unable to locate one, they got on the turnpike and drove toward Louisville. Then, since they were on the way, they decided to drive on in and see her. They stopped on the outskirts of Louisville, where the monk telephoned Margie to ask if it would be all right to come see her. He cautioned her that he was dressed in Trappist overalls and needed a shave. That made no difference.

They found their way to Lourdes Hall. Merton got out and walked around the asphalt parkway looking for her. Two technicians passed without recognizing the monk. Margie, in a brown dress and with her hair flying, came running from one of the entrances. They got into the car, filled with joy to see one another, and headed into a blinding sun trying to find their way to the airport where they hoped to have dinner in the Luau Room.

Despite the monk's appearance, they were admitted. "Lots of rich people were arriving for the Derby and the place was full of brass and money and there I sat, having a marvelous time, looking like a convict . . . satisfied to look at Margie."

After supper, Merton and Margie went off alone, walking aimlessly and talking. They found a couple of trailers parked in a field near the airport buildings and sat in the grass behind them to watch the sunset.

Merton attempted to describe what happened then. "Suppose that the clear light of that evening were love itself, and suppose we just became that light, that love: as if the clear beauty of the evening incarnated itself and its beauty and its meaning in us . . . and the meaning of everything that ever happened was suddenly centered in us because we were now love. It was our turn to express and show forth in worship the essence of all truth and life and meaning by our love."

Merton said that his only truth was in God, it came into being by the call of God, and its true nature had been secret from all but God. The meeting that night had drawn him to reveal his inner depths to Margie, "and now I am known to you and to Him."

They remained alone only a short time, perhaps half an hour, before rejoining James Laughlin and Nicanor Parra to drive back to the hospital.

Afterward, in the darkness, the three men drove silently to the monastery. Merton felt that if Laughlin had misgivings about his part in the meeting, the Chilean poet was simply delighted. "He was saying something about how one must 'follow the ecstasy.' "

That night, in his room in the infirmary, the monk sat up late and wrote a poem about the moments they had spent together at the airport.

The next morning, Laughlin confided affectionately to the monk that although he understood and sympathized with Merton's attachment to Margie, he could not help feeling uneasy about his part in driving the monk to see her. Merton tried to explain the quality and nature and goals of his involvement.

On quite another level, as professional literary men, they discussed the love poems that were flowing from the relationship. Merton thought they might have some value and ought to be kept in a secret file until some later date when they could be reviewed. He asked Laughlin to set up a confidential file, which came to be known as the Menendez file. Merton simply sent his love poems to Laughlin and asked that they go into the "Menendez file." If his mail were opened, it would appear that these were translations of some South American poet.

In a subsequent note to "Dear J.," dated June 9, 1966, Merton wrote:

> Another one for the Menendez file. You will see it continues a part of the series I sent you last time. I cut my finger today and my typing is a bit more erratic than usual. I suppose that if I am rational about it, these Menendez poems will have to remain classified for a long time, even after I die. But anyway, they are there, and life cannot always be fully consistent. Just for the record, all the laws and proprieties are being kept faithfully as far as the strict obligations go.[2]

The next day, Derby Day, Saturday, May 7, Merton awaited the arrival of his friends for the picnic. Dr. Jack Ford and his family were to bring Father John Loftus and Margie. No questions had been asked about her, and Dr. Ford had the general impression that she was perhaps a former nun or someone religiously connected with the monk. The group arrived almost an hour late on a brilliant and cool day that reminded Merton of his ordination day. After the picnic lunch, Merton and Margie went off together knowing it was a foolish imprudence, but unable to resist taking some time alone. They walked to one of Merton's favorite spots beside a small creek. Seated on the mossy bank, Merton read the poem to her. Overwhelmed, they talked for a moment of going away together. But the monk immediately caught himself and explained to her that he was a person who had to live alone, who could not live with anyone else. Margie did not believe him. They discussed the possibility of her getting a job in Louisville, getting a car, and their visiting whenever they could.

When they returned to the picnic area, Merton noted that Gladys Ford gave him some "funny looks" and Father John Loftus was plainly worried.

After listening to the Kentucky Derby together, the visitors left. Merton walked up the hill to his hermitage, awed by the revelations that came to him from Margie's presence. He realized that his own deepest capacities for human love had never before been tapped, and that he too could "love with an awful completeness."

After such moments of tenderness, however, the monk saw clearly that they were being carried implacably into a commitment that threatened to falsify their intentions. In reaction, he resolved to get the matter under control and to state that what was impossible was simply impossible. He struggled to fit his longing for her into the heart of his vocation to solitude, his way of emptiness and unknowing, his inner silence and his Mass, "which is most ardent these days and in which I feel most closely united with her."

Since their friends were reluctant to bring Margie out for picnics, and since Merton himself feared such meetings at the monastery, their visits were limited to his trips into Louisville for medical treatment.

In mid-May the monk had an appointment with Dr. Mitchell, who gave him a painful shot in the left elbow for the bursitis from which he had begun to suffer. He met Margie for lunch at Cunninghams. They sat together in one of the booths and "talked too freely about what we would like to do—vague, unrealistic possibilities."

That evening, in severe pain from the bursitis and the shot, he again sat up late, writing a third love poem entitled "Aubade on a Cloudy Morning," a work filled with intense longing and speculation about their being together.

He awakened in the night, full of anguish. Through the following days his monastic life and work were carried out under the burden of growing anxiety over the impossible contradictions in his life. He spent most of Sunday afternoon walking in the woods and "saw clearly that it can't go on like this. I simply have no business being in love and playing around with a girl, however innocently." The poem "Aubade on a Cloudy Morning" worried him. He felt it was not fitting for a monk. It revealed to him the virtual impossibility of transforming a love now so filled with erotic undercurrents into the purely spiritual union they had envisioned. He concluded that although this was the deepest human relationship he had ever experienced, it must end sooner or later, and that it would be soon.

When he telephoned her that afternoon, she sensed the difference in his tone and was hurt. This added to his self-reproach and so upset him that he abandoned any attempt to work that afternoon.

It could not go on like this. No matter how painful it might be to end it, in the long run it would be better. He would not declare it over—nothing sudden, just a gentle drawing back, an occasional letter, an occasional safe visit.

After another long telephone conversation on Monday, May 17, the monk was totally stymied. He could find no human solution. They had discussed all theoretical possibilities, even the hope of a married clergy. Merton's conscience could no longer tolerate the hidden meetings, the illegal phone calls. They made plans to see one another on Thursday, Ascension Day. He hoped that some solution would be found then.

"We are determined that our love must be spiritual and chaste," Merton wrote, "But the longing for her is frightful — and of course so is the conflict that goes with it."

The monk handled his torments in the way most profoundly natural to him by writing about them. His journals and notebooks of this period scarcely contain anything except speculations about this relationship. The word "impossible" crops up frequently. "All through everything, I come back to the one word 'impossible.' "

Limited in their contacts, they compensated. They settled on a song, Joan Baez's recording of "Silver Dagger," and listened to it and thought of one another whenever they heard it. Also, they set a time of 1:30 A.M., when Margie got off from work. Merton would awaken and they would unite themselves in thought.

The waking hours of his nights became crises of affection for her, flooding him with tears in which he saw her heart "in all its preciousness before God." Merton's tough-mindedness and habitual strength dissolved into a desolating vulnerability during these night awakenings. He wept frequently, sustained only by the vision and the hope that "we will be united at last forever in heaven. But the way there will be terrible, with the anguish and longing we feel for each other."

Margie existed as an invisible presence in his heart. She became part of his sense of a "day" that belonged eternally to them, a day that was not on any calendar, a day of their love, a day that "just goes on and on." He came to see this as a kind of contemplation with its own lights and insights. One of these insights, which Merton considered important, centered around a new understanding of the place of sexual love in Hinduism.

A nurse friend drove Margie out to the abbey on Ascension Day, May 19 and returned later to take her back to Louisville. Merton met them on the side of the road. He and Margie walked off into the woods at the foot of the Vineyard Knobs, loaded with picnic supplies. Margie carried a bag of food dripping with some ice that cooled the sauterne. They could not go far because the wet sack was coming to pieces.

In a secluded spot, they ate herring and ham and drank the wine. Merton read poems and they talked, pledging themselves to make the sacrifice of all physical consolations even while "nature placidly and inexorably said something more profound and perhaps inevitable."

Merton did not delude himself over this profound physical attraction. Instead of feeling impure, he wrote, he felt purified. He was actually quoting from himself, from an article he had written a few days earlier in "Seven Words," a collection edited by Ned O'Gorman. It seemed somehow healthy and right because they really did "belong to each other in our love." But he immediately noted in parenthesis: "(bad argument — it could justify anything)."

Always, in the end, Merton had to come back to the "enormous, unthinkable problem of my vow and dedication which really come first and make the whole thing absurdly impossible."

As frequently happened in those days, Merton's ecstatic reaction to their meeting fluctuated toward the opposite direction by the next afternoon. His conscience tormented him. His nerves were shattered. If the day before he felt they completed one another and welcomed as healthy his longing for physical consummation, he now was offended by that image of himself, impatient with sensual consolation, "backing away from domination by it, suspicious of its tyranny," and turning with all his energies toward freedom. He loved her, but did not want to think of her. He wanted to get back to work, to write his conference for the next Sunday, to read and meditate and "get the heaviness of passion" off his mind. Once again he wanted to eat. For the first time in two months he had an appetite.

On Sunday evening, May 22, Merton was sufficiently recovered from his surgery to leave the infirmary and move back into the hermitage on a full-time basis. The first night showed him again his profound need for solitude and his inability to be truly himself anywhere except in solitude. He sat on the porch and let the night absorb him, watching fireflies among the pines and tracing Scorpius' rise over trees in the silence.

The next morning he got up long before dawn and resumed his regular schedule of reading and some manual work, though his back was still sore. "There is no question at all that this is right for me," he wrote. "I am a solitary and that's that." He affirmed that his purpose in life was to live as God would have him live — a life of aloneness and freedom, unconnected, with nothing to gain and nothing to lose, and with nothing to explain.

In this mood he walked down to the abbey to pick up his mail. It contained prints of photographs he had taken of her May 5. He found them charming, but did not spend much time looking at them. "Our love is on a certain level serious . . . but there is something more serious yet, and that is freedom from all special design or particular project." Nevertheless, he telephoned her to discover that she had made plans to come and spend part of the day with him on May 30. Merton suggested they "skip it," to which she replied, "Well, what do you *mean?*" The monk felt he could no longer bear the complications and fears, even for the great joy of being with her. He wrote in his journal that "there is this involved and complex machinery of love one has to get into, with all its wheels within wheels, this leading to that and that implying this. What do I want with such a snarled up ball of string?"

This did not imply any diminution of love. On the contrary, their passion for one another had now reached a point where it was almost intolerable. He feared it would simply overwhelm them if they were ever alone for any length of time again. He was a priest, a monk for twenty-five years. He had given up that kind of joy and he reproached himself for having allowed the relationship to get as deep as it had.

But what could he do about it now? He foresaw that it would probably continue as it was, with moments of anguish, passion and joy. "Better settle down wisely and peacefully to a long struggle in which we sweat out our passion and (if possible) simmer down to a peaceful, loving, lasting friendship that will sustain our affection for years to come."

On May 27 Merton wrote her that the only answer was sacrifice. If they were willing to love each other in a spirit of true sacrifice, their love would endure and deepen and be consecrated to God.

They decided, nevertheless, to try to see one another again on an illegal visit, but Margie could not get transportation. Merton, though disappointed, was relieved. Another visit would have led to too much anguish, too much struggle. What struck Merton most was the waste of spiritual energy involved in their torments, a waste that prevented him from giving "everything I have to my real task."

Margie went home to see her family on Saturday, the Vigil of Pentecost. That afternoon, the monk took a long walk out on the ridge of St. Edmund's field, where he spent the afternoon in the sun. For the first time since going to the hospital, he felt some of his former peace and freedom—"a sense of having no worries in the world and nothing to take too seriously because I don't have to take myself seriously." With Margie some distance away and out of possible communication, Merton discovered that he could again be free, "that freedom is right there if only I want it, and believe me, I want it! Today I see that I have been a very great damned fool. . . . This is not Margie's fault—she just loves me, but that is sufficient reason for me to be a damned fool, I suppose."

Although constantly preoccupied with his emotional involvement, Father Louis continued on the surface to lead a life normal to him as a world-renowned religious, concerned with the problems of humanity, in contact with many people by mail and a few by visits.

On the Vigil of the Pentecost, Saturday afternoon and evening he spent some hours with a man whom he vastly admired, the Vietnamese Buddhist monk and poet Thich Nhat Hanh. Both men had been monks about the same length of time, though Nhat Hanh had entered the monastery much younger, at the age of sixteen. Merton described the visitor as a completely formed monk, a quiet, humble, simple, direct man. Both men were intellectuals and poets. They quickly came to view one another as brothers.

The next afternoon, May 29, in his regular Sunday conference for the community, Father Merton talked about Nhat Hanh and his long Zen Buddhist formation, his heroic opposition to the continuing war in his country, and his poetry. Father Louis destroyed the myth that Buddhists are anti-life. On the contrary, their training and formation build in them profound respect for life and for the living, growing things created by God; he compared their spirituality in this sense to the Franciscan spirituality in the West.

The monks at Gethsemani were most interested in Nhat Hanh's training in meditation. Father Louis had asked him about this, and shared his response. At first Buddhist monks are not allowed to meditate, the visitor had explained. Before you can meditate, you've got to learn not to slam doors.

The Trappists responded with spontaneous laughter. Merton expanded on the point. What sense did it make to go around slamming doors and trying to meditate? What sense did it make going around banging things, making noise, acting in an uncontrolled manner and then for a half-hour each day trying to recollect oneself and meditate?

The goal of this formation was not to teach men to meditate, but to teach them to live, to form the whole person so that all aspects of life become ordered, tranquil and quiet. Then, what is within can develop.

Both men had lost brothers in wars. Father Louis, who had written so eloquently of his own brother's death in the poem "For My Brother," now read Nhat Hanh's lines on the death of his brother entitled "Peace":

> They woke me this morning
> To tell me my brother had been killed in battle.
> Yet in the garden, uncurling moist petals,
> A new rose blooms on the bush.
> And I am alive, can still breathe the fragrance of roses
>   and dung,
> Eat, pray and sleep.
> But when can I break my long silence.
> When can I speak the unuttered words that are choking
>   me?[3]

June

As soon as Margie returned to Louisville the following Tuesday the phone calls were resumed. Despite themselves, they got "deeper and deeper in love." For the monk, the most satisfactory call occurred on Saturday. Margie agreed again that under no circumstance must he be unfaithful to his vows. She challenged him on a point he made about "detachment." He conceded that it was nonsense to talk about detachment when you were in love, and made a frank commitment: he was attached to her, and moreover this attachment profoundly changed his life.

"More or less clear-sightedly," Merton wrote that evening, "I am taking a course that can be harmful to me as a monk, as a contemplative, and as a writer." He stipulated, however, that this attachment had to remain in harmony with his vows, and if it did not, then he would "have to abide by the vows."

The questions of regularity, observance and discipline had to be resolved and the monk made the effort. He felt he was getting back into his hermit life. He was reading better, meditating a little but not well. Most of his thoughts were about her. He anticipated being up a little late that night thinking about her and asking himself a lot of questions. "So many other priests are doing the same thing tonight—everywhere. It is a strange crisis in the whole Church."

Later, after reading Camus, Merton meditated on his situation and deduced, in line with Camus's thought, "my tragedy turns out to be the evidence of my inner disposition to mediocrity disguised in a religious ideal." He reflected that whatever might be right or wrong about his love for Margie, the experience showed him something important: the true relationship was not between her and his ideal self, but between her and his actual and real self; and he must be grateful if that ideal self was from time to time discredited by his own "stupidity and selfishness."

This dissonance between the ideal self and the actual self burdened the monk. It occurred in almost all of his contacts. He acknowledged that he had helped create this ideal self through his writings and his reputation as a religious recluse, though a great deal of it came from the popular image of "men of God." With people for whom he felt spontaneous sympathy and friendship, Merton tried to erase that ideal self, usually with blunt and earthy language. To assume the mask of the ideal self represented delusion and falsity to him. He loathed occasions where such conformity was forced on him, and he welcomed, almost as a relief, occasions that clarified his truth by discrediting the ideal self.

One of the greatest blessings of the hermit life was liberation from this implicit demand that he measure up to others' expectations. This in turn lessened his concern over a danger common to spiritual people—the danger of a subtle, pervading delusion that can insinuate itself into those who are so often reminded of the ideal self that they come to believe in that as the truth, lose touch with their own reality and thereby forfeit all hope of being truly free. Merton had no doubts about his capacity to live up to the expectations, "all foolish" of an ideal self. "Of course I can't. I must manfully face this judgment and find my center not in an ideal self which just *is* (fully realized) but in actual self which does all it can to be honest and to love truly, though it still may fail."

In those weeks Merton was able to suffer all the anguish and torments of love and simultaneously stand aside and observe himself in an almost relentless manner. Finally Margie had to ask him to stop analyzing the relationship, since she felt he ran the risk of misunderstanding her. He agreed but found it impossible to avoid the most detailed speculation in an attempt to understand his position.

What distressed and fascinated him was the way in which his strong resolutions simply melted the moment he saw her or spoke with her on the telephone. Instead of finding, as he had so confidently anticipated, that this human love could be integrated into his monastic and priestly vocation, he found he was, in effect, leading a dual life.

Two days later one of the monks drove him to Louisville for another bursitis shot and they set a time to meet later in the afternoon for the trip back to Gethsemani. Margie met him, they found a quiet spot and held on to their moments together so long that Merton did not arrive back for his ride until almost an hour late. "I wonder what all my resolutions and reasonings amount to!" he wrote after his return.

After a night of fitful sleep Merton awakened on the morning of June 12 with the calm realization that they could not go on as they were. It was not only a question of his vows. It was his certainty that this was the right life for him, the only life for him, and that he was jeopardizing everything. "I want the life I have vowed . . . I have to try to live the life I have chosen." The preceding afternoon had proved again that his resolves did not hold when he was with Margie. "Therefore we can't meet alone." He affirmed his love for her; he loved her more than he had ever loved anyone in his life. But now he was convinced that this love could bring only suffering and disaster to both of them unless they found the strength to change its course. Margie would accept any terms. Her intention to unite their love to his religious vocation was as strong as his. When they were together, however, past and future intentions were obliterated in wild intensity of the instant.

On June 13, the abbot returned from his trip. That evening Merton went down to the steel building to use the telephone. There, one of the monks informed him that the brother on duty at the gatehouse switchboard had seen a light on one of the circuits late one previous night and had plugged in to determine if the phone were off the hook. He had overheard some of Merton's call to Margie and had reported the matter to the abbot.

Merton did not know how much he had heard or which call had been intercepted. In any event, Merton knew that the abbot was now aware of at least some of the details, "and is waiting to give me the devil about it, which is only natural."

Though troubled almost to the point of panic, Merton was swept with a sense of relief that the matter was now in the open. From this viewpoint of openness, his own perspective changed. He told himself he had to face the fact that he had been wrong. "Much as I love Margie, I should never have let myself be carried away and become so utterly imprudent."

Both of them had anticipated this. The danger of discovery, the primacy of Merton's vows, the knowledge that each visit or call could be the last had added to the intensity of their moments together.

Merton understood that it was "clearly over now."

He called to tell her what had happened. "She was frantic and so was I."

She said, "I had the most terrible feeling something was wrong when I was waiting for you to call . . . will we ever see each other again? . . . What will I do without you? . . . How unfair it is, how inhuman."

Despite his turmoil, Merton continued to view the abbot's discovery as a help. He felt he had fallen into real spiritual danger and that matters had "really got close to going wrong." Dr. Wygal had warned him only the Sunday before, "Be careful you don't destroy yourself." Merton now saw that his friend was more right than he had thought at the time. The abbot's discovery might very well be providential in saving him from a wreck.

The next day, when the abbot had not summoned him, Merton decided to "own up and face Dom James." The abbot displayed no anger. He was kind and attempted to be understanding. Although sympathizing warmly with Merton, the abbot demanded a complete break as the only possible solution. He offered to write the young lady, whose identity he did not yet know. Merton declined. The abbot's understanding did not coincide with Merton's. He hinted that Merton's loneliness in the hermitage had led to this. In utter dread of losing the solitary life, Merton explained he had met Margie when he was in pain and sedated and therefore without defenses. The abbot could not be shaken from his loneliness theory. He suggested the monk continue to live in the hermitage during the day, but sleep in the infirmary at night. Merton asked to be allowed to remain in the hermitage full time. Finally the abbot agreed on the condition that Merton come down for ecumenical work at the retreat house—as a means of mitigating his loneliness.

Beneath the essentially pain-filled overtones of that meeting, the abbot's solution struck Merton as funny. Here he was gaunt with the emotional ravages of love and the abbot advised solving his problem by talking to ecumenical groups. "A cure for loneliness!" Merton wrote.

After saying Vespers in the hermitage, relieved to have salvaged at least his hermit-life, Merton "walked in the silent grass and looked at the clouds," and found all the essence of his love for Margie there. He thought of her loneliness and prayed that she might be filled with this same grace of acceptance, peace and deep union he experienced now that the inevitability of separation was clear.

That evening he sank into his pain, torn with sorrow for Margie, who must be suffering those hours. His own loneliness was magnified by a sense of alienation from the community. He imagined falsely that his situation was generally known and that he was a pariah among his brothers, alone, "like a solitary stone." Did not the abbot's secretary avert his eyes in embarrassment when they met? And the gatehouse brother smiled much too politely. "I am known as a monk in love with a woman."

During a difficult and tormented night of dreams and frequent wakenings, Merton allowed himself to drift to the very heart of loneliness, dimly aware of the long hours in the darkness of the hermitage, in the stillness and silence of the surrounding forest, until the loneliness was total and desolate of every human consolation. He waited, abandoning himself to the emptiness, until loneliness transformed itself into solitude and he realized it was right for him. He welcomed the return of a solitude that nourished him and that he had not known for months.

He awakened hollow from lack of sleep but feeling more himself.

"In order to untie a knot you must first find out how the knot was tied. Buddha." He began his journal notes. He wrote that for the first time since entering the hospital he knew real inner freedom and solitude. "I love M. but in a different way, peacefully and without disturbance or inner division. I feel that once again I am all here. I have finally returned to my place and to my work and am beginning to be once again what I am. It has been a time of gruesome yet beautiful alienation."

That day he read again. He finished Tucker's *Philosophy and Myth in Karl Marx*, which he considered good material for conferences. But behind everything he needed to know how Margie was feeling. If he could only be assured that she was all right, that her job, her activities and her human contacts were making it bearable for her, he would be truly at peace.

That afternoon Dr. Wygal appeared unexpectedly and they discussed the "problem." They took a drive to nearby New Haven. Merton persuaded the doctor to let him attempt a call to Margie on the car telephone. That attempt failed. Dr. Wygal warned him not to get back on a "collision course." Merton assured him he wanted only to get matters settled and straight. In New Haven, the monk tried to phone again and reached her at the hospital. Both were overjoyed. Merton was relieved to hear she was all right, though she spoke of her terrible loneliness. She assured him she loved him more than ever. He was able to give her some practical information about the abbot's prohibitions. He told her it would be useless to write him at the abbey or to try to contact him in any direct way. After the call when Merton glowed with happiness, the doctor warned him again. Merton agreed with the doctor but insisted it was a question now of tapering off gradually and mercifully.

Although he still had trouble sleeping, and moments of nearly unbearable nervous crisis, the monk had the gift of simply waiting them out, in observing them and learning from them.

"The bitter and lucid joys of solitude," he wrote on June 18. "The real desert is this: to face the real limitations of one's own existence and knowledge and not try to manipulate them or disguise them. Not to embellish them with possibilities." He believed that in solitude when accurate limitations were seen and accepted they vanished and new dimensions opened up. The present was unlimited. But the only way to grasp it in its unlimitedness was to remove limitations placed on it by future expectations or regrets about the past. Margie felt that when he accepted being alone it implied a rejection of her, that he was thrusting her out of his present, his solitude. But he could not reject her and saw no reason even for attempting it. The idea of a perfect, empty solitude now seemed preposterous. Solitude existed only in the frail mortal human person facing his own true present. Merton saw his own true present as one in which Margie was loved as a value of great mystery. She asked that the monk retain a place in his solitude in which she would always be known. He would not refuse this. "It is the root of my commitment and my fidelity to give her this anchor in my sea of loneliness."

Father Louis meditated on the Camus principle that the "absurd" man is without human hope, and that his hopelessness isolates him in the pure present. The monk in refusing to "contaminate my acceptance by inserting into it imaginary hopes," realized that he differed from Camus in the immense unknown hope that was his own aspect of the "absurd." His hope did not spring, he said, from knowledge or stoicism but from faith. He possessed "his spirit of stark adoration . . . which is another aspect of the absurd and the absolute."

That afternoon Carolyn and Victor Hammer drove from Lexington for a visit. Merton took them down into the woods for a picnic, the same place he had gone with Margie on Derby Day. He told his old friends about his situation. They understood better than anyone, he said, except Nicanor Parra. However, like Merton's other friends, they agreed that the attachment had reached a dead end and the only thing to do was to accept the fact.

When the Hammers left Merton picked up his mail and returned in the late afternoon to his hermitage. He took particular strength from one of the letters. His old friend Eleanor Duckett, a professor at Smith College and an authority on monasticism, wrote of her delight in the kind of life he had been given, that in the world today there should be those willing to live in real solitude.

"This is important to me," the monk noted. "For she knows what monasticism is and she respects the *reality* of monastic solitude. Seeing it through her eyes, I am deeply moved by the meaning of this strange life."

Father Louis added that in many ways he had not been truly faithful to the solitary life. Yet who could say what were its real demands other than those who had to meet them? And who could know what were the failures and problems of those forgotten people who lived as solitaries in the past? How many of them were lonely and in love? The stories of the Desert Fathers contained material about such things.

> All I know is that here I am, and the valley is very quiet, the sun is going down, there is no human being around and as darkness falls I could easily be a completely forgotten person, as if I did not exist for the world at all. The day could easily come when I would be just as invisible as if I never existed, and still be living here on this hill. And I would be perfectly content to be so.

At eight o'clock, with the first stars appearing in a twilight sky, the monk went into the back sleeping room of his cabin, undressed and lay on his cot. His arm and back ached. He lay there at the edge of sleep, unable to sleep, allowing images to rise to the surface of his consciousness. He imagined that Margie might be on her way to him, though she had never seen the hermitage and could not possibly find it in the dark. If only he heard a soft knock on the door, and opened it to see her standing on the porch. Unable to bear his vision, Merton got up, dressed and walked in front of the hermitage. He wandered toward the forest path that leads down to the abbey, tempted to try telephoning her. He caught himself, shook off the idea and walked back to the cabin. He emptied his thoughts of everything except the reality of the moment — the vast silence of the woods full of fireflies and stars. No light from any house or farm penetrated the darkness.

Merton sat on the porch and deliberately refused to rationalize anything, to explain anything or to comment on anything. "Only what is there. I am there. Fireflies, stars, darkness, the massive shadows of the woods, the vague dark valley. And nothing, nothing, nothing."

He waited, fixing his attention to the south on the huge sign of the Scorpion and the red eye of Regulus, until the nothingness filled with a sense of presence, totality and peace. Nothing became everything.

"I think of going back to bed, in peace without knowing why, a peace that cannot be justified by anything, any reason, any proof, any argument, any supposition. There are no suppositions left."

The monk walked inside to his sleeping room, knelt by the bed and gazed at the ikon of the nativity that hung on the pitted grey concrete-tile wall dimly illuminated by lamplight.

"What is there to look for or to yearn for but *all* reality here and now in whatever I am?" Merton wrote.

The following morning, in making his notes, Merton remarked how difficult it was to write of such an experience without adding rationalizations and explanations, or trying to capture God in mere words. Because of the limitations of language the monk felt it was disastrous to speak of God. Yet not to speak of God meant that nothing could be said about his experience of the night before.

" 'Who is like unto God?' The secret of knowing that there is none like Him and of disposing my whole thought and being in accordance with this secret. The long labor of getting back to the center."

That Sunday afternoon, June 19, Merton went down to the abbey to give his weekly conference. He hurried back after supper to get away from the temptation to telephone Margie.

His night was similar to those preceding nights when he would retire at his regular time, become restless with pain and longing for Margie and finally get up and write or read. He said it did not really matter. He loved the loneliness of the night. It taught him to view solitude as act, and to conclude that the reason no one really understood solitude was because people viewed it as a condition, something one elected to undergo — like standing under a shower. Actually, solitude was for him a realization, even a kind of creation as well as a liberation of active forces within him. As a mere condition, solitude could be passive, inert and basically unreal: a kind of coma. To avoid this condition, he had to work actively at solitude.

Thus, the need for discipline, for techniques of integration that keep body and soul together, harmonizing their powers to bring them into one deep resonance oriented to the root of being.

Freedom began for Father Louis with the willingness to realize and experience his life as totally absurd in relation to the apparent meaning which has been thrown over life by society and by illusions. But that could be only a starting point leading to a deeper realization of that root reality in himself and in all life *"which I do not know and cannot know . . . This implies the capacity to see that realizing and knowing are not the same . . . —solitude itself is the fullness of realization. In solitude I become fully able to realize what I cannot know."*

At midnight, June 21, Merton awakened convinced that someone was knocking lightly on the door of the hermitage. Again he suffered the desire to go down and attempt a call, but this time he lectured himself severely. It was not a matter of just being "found out," but a question of a deeper responsibility. He regarded his vocation certainly as more than a matter of being in a certain place and wearing a certain kind of costume. Too many people in the world relied on the fact that he was serious about deepening an inner dimension of experience that they desired but that was closed to them. It was not closed to the monk. "This is a gift that has been given me not for myself, but for everyone. I cannot let it be squandered and dissipated foolishly. It would be criminal to do so."

He slept and awoke to a cool brilliant morning. Bird songs filled the forest and the valley was full of sunlit mist. Tall daylilies were opening in the June sun. The monk knew he was where he belonged. Books and papers were on his table and work was waiting. He knew the poets he must read. For the first time he was getting into Louis Zukofsky, "who is certainly one of the great classic poets of our time. Great mastery and richness and structure."

Everything harmonized in solitude. Only there could the monk be himself. He felt that the real wrong lay in playing roles and taking them seriously. He did not take any role too seriously, but still, he had to play roles in order to communicate with people. "The beauty of the solitary life, trees that say nothing and skies that are neutral, is that you can throw away all the masks and forget them until you return among people."

On the night of June 24 Merton dreamed he saw a tangle of dark briars and light roses. His attention fixed on one beautiful pink rose, which became luminous in a way that revealed the silk texture of its petals. His mother's face appeared behind the roses and the roses vanished.

The next morning, exactly three months after the operation, Merton prepared to go for x-rays of his back. He was not supposed to see Margie but he had sent out a brief note to be mailed by one of his visitors. He promised himself that if she did come to the doctor's office, they would have a clear understanding that they must not see each other again, and that the monk could not write or call. He felt an almost desperate need to get back to what he believed he ought to be as far as discipline was concerned. That morning, before leaving, he had made a beginning by reading the Gospel of Mark. "Very moved by the first ten or fifteen lines. So I begin again."

Merton got his x-rays quickly and learned that his back had healed but he had another deteriorated disc. This, however, posed no immediate problems.

Since Margie was not there, Merton went down in the elevator. On the ground floor, she was waiting to get in as he got out. Together they went back to the fourth floor and sat alone in the hall by the window, "talking, deeply moved, torn with sorrow." She told him that in view of the abbot's attitude, and Dr. Wygal's agreement with it, she could no longer bear to work in Louisville and had made application for a job in Cincinnati.

Merton insisted that Margie accompany him and Dr. Wygal to lunch at Cunninghams. In spite of Dr. Wygal's obvious disapproval, Merton said he and Margie enjoyed themselves, talking and laughing and playing their favorite recordings.

Dr. Wygal left to take care of some errands. As soon as they were alone the two "fell on each other in desperation and love . . . swept with love and lost in it, knowing it would probably never be like that again."

When the doctor returned, they drove Margie to St. Joseph's. The monk watched her vanish through glass doors into the shadows and wondered if he would ever see her again.

The meeting made it impossible for the monk to sleep that night. At eleven he abandoned the attempt, got up and paced the length of his porch until after one A.M. He slept fitfully from one until five A.M. when he got up and said Lauds. He breakfasted on strong black tea and rye bread. In the early dawn he renewed his intention to obey the commands given him and he pronounced any further active relationship "all over. And that is how it has to be."

By the end of June the monk was beginning to make some progress on what he called the "true road." He wrote her what he hoped was his last letter, struggling to keep out any commitment to meet her at any special time in Louisville. This he finally accomplished, but only after destroying page after page. Thus he was left free of any need to worry about future meetings. They could be avoided. It would be better that way, though terribly difficult, but the monk felt that the sacrifice was demanded.

To get back into authentic solitude he would have to rebuild his life. "The state I am in now is quite appalling, as if I had lost everything," he wrote. "And yet I trust in God's grace, and feel that though I have proved once again that I am totally absurd and helpless when left to myself, He, nevertheless has secretly remained with me and is supporting me."

Merton identified once more with the opening of the Gospel of Mark in which is described Jesus' forty days in the wilderness and his temptation. But Merton saw the past three months also as an experience that had opened his depths and perhaps given him his first real perception of love and the affective nature at the human level.

By June 29, the monk was able to get a good night's sleep. He got up at three and made what he termed "a halfway decent meditation," while "dirty rain frothed off the roof into the buckets like beer."

After breakfast, with the rain still pouring, he noticed a difference in his inner climate. He was no longer singing "Silver Dagger" but rather the French children's song *"Sur le Pont d'Avignon."*

Father Louis returned to Eckhart, who had been his "life-raft" in the hospital. He copied "Blessed are the pure in heart who leave everything to God now as they did before they ever existed," and prayed that he could get back to that spirit.

July

While he appeared to be making a good return to his life as a monk and hermit, temptations to see Margie assaulted him. He called the first week of July a week of excesses in which he wrote and destroyed many letters to her. He felt some satisfaction when at last he did not give in to the temptation to get up at night and write to her or about her. He remarked that it was "instructive to see how easily I am shaken and thrown off balance," and how much work remained to be done before he got steady again.

Reviewing the past weeks, the monk recognized how much he had been deluded and how much he had wanted to be deluded, "because there is such a great good in human love, and I needed this good, or thought I did. Well, I did. But I needed to know that I was called to something else. And the fact that I risked my other and special calling now frightens me."

Father Abbot sent Merton to see Father John Eudes, the psychiatrist at the abbey. Though Father Louis was embarrassed that the two men had discussed him, his sessions with Father Eudes helped fortify him in his determination to live his solitary life. He was also reassured that the community was fully behind him and wishing him well.

Struggling to stabilize himself, the monk grasped those moments when clarity came to him. On July 12 he sat before dawn in the dim light of his porch and looked out at the peaceful valley. "I realized that no matter how much I may love Margie and be attached to her, there has never for a moment really been any choice."

The next day, July 13, Dr. Wygal came to spend the day, one of the hottest days Merton could remember. The heat rendered him heavy and stupid. The two men sought relief from the torpor by driving around in Dr. Wygal's car. At noon they picked up some hamburgers at Reilly's in Bardstown. In the early afternoon, Merton wanted to call Margie on the phone, but Dr. Wygal refused to cooperate.

Later, around two, in the full heat of afternoon, they stopped by the motherhouse of the Sisters of Loretto in nearby Nerinx where they hoped to see Sister Luke Tobin. Sister Luke was absent, but the two friends remained to visit with the other sisters.

One of them noted that Merton wore a baggy pair of blue jean work pants with a sweaty matching jacket and a black triangular neckerchief that resembled a cowl.

They sat in a room and talked. One of the sisters asked Merton about the hermit life. He remarked that one should not attempt to verbalize that kind of life, but he would try to say a few things about his external existence. He emphasized how much freedom a hermit has. A hermit must be content just to be, to exist, to have a life totally different from the life of anyone else. Gradually, in solitude a person comes to grips with certain essentials. I am I. God is God. Life is Life.

He spoke of the more fruitful moments when he waited for it to make sense, such as the time two nights before when it was so hot he could not sleep. He paced the front room of his hermitage for three hours, barefoot and in shorts, and "some of the answers came."

The conversation turned to Dr. Daisetz T. Suzuki, whom Merton considered one of the finest Zen philosophers. The monk mentioned Suzuki's death and asked the sisters to pray for him. He told them that when he met with Suzuki both men brought materials to share. Dr. Suzuki picked up a Portuguese poem Merton wanted him to see because it resembled Zen. The elderly scholar read aloud: "Thank God I am *no* good," and was so delighted he repeated the line again. His secretary thought she had not heard correctly but was told, "Yes, thank God I am no good."

The sisters persuaded Merton to talk about Zen. He told them religiously oriented people almost always convince themselves that they are special, an attitude that separates them from others. They tend to set up an "ideal-self" in opposition to an "actual-self" and then waste energy coping with the false problems that arise. Often these false problems can be the excuse they fabricate to explain the gap between "what I am" and "what I think I should be," which gives rise to the constant need for self-justification.

Father Louis touched on Zen practices that help clarify this notion of false problems. A Zen practitioner is given a problem by his master and must report each day on his solution. Merton confided the problem he was attempting to resolve. You have a young goose in a bottle. The goose grows too large for the bottle. How do you remove the goose without killing it or breaking the bottle? The idea, he explained, was to concentrate so intensely on this problem that everything else fades to insignificance.

The practitioner takes his solution to the master each day only to learn that he has not found the solution. Eventually he comes to realize that the solution to the problem is simply that there is no solution so why bother looking for one. The monk said he was seated in choir one day during a solemn profession when he suddenly thought, "Of course, the goose swallowed the bottle." He had seen finally that it was stupid to try to find a reasonable solution to the problem because the problem did not have to be solved; any solution would do.

They asked him if all problems were false. What about people starving?

That was a real problem, Merton agreed. But we must make certain to see it as it is. Are we looking for the first step to take regarding these starving people, or are we looking for what we should do to appear liberal or just? The latter would obscure the real problem with a false one, which must be abandoned. False problems center on oneself. Real problems concern everyone. The only solution to the false problem, he said, is to conclude that we do not have to solve it.

When the monk mentioned his love for music, the group persuaded Sister Jeremy to play some Debussy and Gershwin for him. He remarked that she played very well indeed, and he enjoyed it, but he felt uneasy about having talked so much and so glibly.

The continuing unrelieved heat of July was depleting to the monk. He experienced the erosion of his resolve to obey what he felt were correct restrictions placed on him by his abbot. In the guise of being merciful to Margie, of charity and responsibility, he smuggled out letters by his friends and visitors, most of whom simply mailed them without any knowledge that this was an evasion.

His next appointment with Dr. Mitchell was scheduled for July 16. He got word to Margie, but was not sure she would meet him. While waiting to go in, once he had notified her, he fell into a state of "anxious, disoriented consciousness, making erratic and desperate acts, calling on God, trying to recover orientation, thinking of Margie, questioning self, fearing consequences of imprudence."

Margie came to the doctor's office in a taxicab and they went for a picnic in Cherokee Park. Merton described it as one of the most beautiful and untroubled times they had had together.

But as always, he reacted afterward by falling into depression and disgust with himself, remaining disoriented and unable to work until July 20. Then it turned cooler and he found the strength to begin his introduction to John Wu's book *The Golden Age of Zen,* even though he did not feel as though he were ready for that yet.

That same day he accepted Ed Rice's proposal that he write an article on Bob Dylan for *Jubilee.* Rice said he would send along some Dylan records for research purposes.

The next day, revising some notes on monastic life, the monk read through the Council decree *Perfectae Caritatis,* and was deeply impressed by these lines: "Through the profession of obedience, religious offer to God a total dedication of their own wills as a sacrifice of themselves; they thereby unite themselves with greater steadiness and security to the saving will of God."[4]

Merton found this "very clear and helpful," and noted that he had been evading this. Now he needed to hear and take it to heart. He reasoned that his love for Margie entailed certain obligations to her, but admitted he had been too willing to disobey in order to contact and console her. Now, he was committed to see her one more time before she left to take up her work in Cincinnati. But that should end it. Merton prayed for the grace to let it end, convinced that this "union with the saving will of God" would benefit her even more than himself.

They planned a final meeting in Louisville for August 12, the day before Margie's graduation from nursing school and also the day of Merton's next appointment with his doctors.

The tensions aroused in Father Louis by this deliberate plan, coupled with extreme pain from his bursitis, drove him to abandon the idea of seeing Margie again. He found the strength to change his appointment to an earlier date and to obey the command not to see her or let her know he was coming into town. In addition to the bursitis, he was beginning to be troubled with numbness in his left leg, for which he also made an appointment to see Dr. Marshall, the neurosurgeon.

Merton sent Margie a letter saying they would have to call off their meeting for the twelfth, and in effect telling her good-bye. As soon as it was mailed, he felt it was heartless to terminate their relationship in this curt manner and he attempted to telephone her, but without success.

The trip into Louisville was a troublesome one for Merton. He had a cortisone shot in the morning for the bursitis, then went to lunch with Dr. Wygal and in the afternoon he kept his appointment with Dr. Marshall, who could do nothing for the numbness.

In Dr. Marshall's office the monk felt so "torn by loneliness and longing to talk to her" that he was almost "visibly crying." As he was being driven back to the abbey on the turnpike, passing near the hospital, he could scarcely bear his anguish. He recited the office all the while feeling "silent cries come slowly tearing and rending their way up out of the very ground of my being." The starkness of his grief frightened him, but he could do nothing about "these metaphysical howls."

Only when he got back into the silence of his hermitage did they finally subside. That night he wrote a poem he had begun to scribble while at the Medical Arts Building, "A Blues for Margie," which he described as "a sort of Bob Dylan thing."

August

His conferences with Father John Eudes continued into early August, and even though it was painful for Merton to air his difficulties, he recognized how helpful these talks were. After one of them, he wrote: "It certainly has done something to get me to *decide* clearly for solitude, and that is the important thing. I am really relieved at not having to continue that complex double game of letters, phone calls and so forth. No trouble admitting this was all wrong. Not just a matter of external correctness, but of inner unity and consistency."

On Sunday, August 7, a Day of Recollection, the monk went to confession to Father Flavian, who told him that people were wondering what was the matter with him and if he might be having difficulties with the abbot. At Mass Merton reflected on how far he had failed in meekness and non-violence: not the external acceptance, but the interior surrender to peace, particularly in relation to the abbot's injunctions.

After Mass he walked in a broad open field on the east farm, watched the high clouds and said aloud the word "desolation" to hear how it sounded. Then he read in *The Book of the Poor in Spirit* how a human being comes to God by many deaths.

The next morning Merton began to receive letters about selections from *Conjectures of a Guilty Bystander* that were appearing in *Life* Magazine along with the first mass-publication of photos of the hermit (August 5, 1966). Merton had not seen the issue though he knew it was to be published since *Life* had paid a considerable fee for the rights. The abbot also knew but he reproached Merton for these "non-hermit" activities. The monk was not certain if this was because of the *Life* article or his unauthorized visit with the Loretto Sisters in mid-July.

On August 12, the day Merton and Margie had planned a final picnic in Cherokee Park and then cancelled it, the Father Abbot agreed to allow Merton to make a commitment or "profession" as a hermit, and they set the date for September 8. Merton looked forward to this for many reasons. First, he viewed it as a way toward deeper consecration to God. Second, no other life interested him, and this meant stabilizing himself officially and formally in the hermit state. Also, he was relieved that he and the abbot were in agreement, "and that there will be no more strain and tension (I hope) over my misdeeds."

The next day Merton awakened at three fifteen to the clatter of rain on the hermitage. He said his Mass early, recalling that this was Margie's graduation day. He affirmed his love for her and expressed gratitude for the few times they had had together. He missed her terribly, he said, but he was at peace and glad he had not attempted to carry through the picnic the day before. He viewed it as a gift, later in the morning, when clusters of delicate mauve lilies, almost like orchids, suddenly bloomed in front of the hermitage — from bulbs Eileen Curns had sent the winter before.

The Victor Hammers came to discuss some publishing projects with Merton. Because of the downpour they sat in the tobacco barn on bales of straw. They told the monk that James Laughlin was worried about him and that they were "glad the affair with Margie was all over."

However, Merton continued to suffer agonizing crises of loneliness and desire to be in touch with her. He remarked after her departure for the new job in Cincinnati that he still thought of her almost constantly.

Letters about the *Life* article continued to arrive. Merton doubted the wisdom of having published in such a mass-circulation magazine, but he was glad for Margie's sake that it had appeared since it gave another contact of sorts and certainly it pleased her and made her proud.

The bursitis became so painful Merton could no longer type. On August 19 he was driven into Louisville for an examination and a cortisone shot. The doctor believed surgery could be avoided. Merton ardently hoped so because another stay in the hospital would certainly involve visits from Margie and the sacrifice of what little peace he had gained. Even if he found the strength not to notify her, her nurse friends surely would.

While in town he made a long-distance call to Margie in Cincinnati. The conversation was "wonderful and in a way shattering. Her voice was full of choked-up emotion."

She had sent him several letters, none of which had reached him. She told him of her plans to come to Louisville to take an exam in late October.

The monk rode back to the abbey assuaged to have talked with her, but also troubled. She would expect him to find some pretext to see her in late October. His own affections would drive him to find that pretext. Wounds that had hardly begun to heal now risked being reopened. Firm resolves now risked being shattered. His distress spilled over into all he saw and heard in the city, into a sense of having encountered miasma in the city's fury, traffic jams, sadism on the radio, and confusion. He returned to the woods "as though wildly plague-stricken, hoping my awareness and suffering are a good sign and they promise recovery."

By August 21, the uneasiness was again resolved in reading Eckhart and in a peaceful sunny afternoon with a sky full of white and blue cumulus clouds. He concluded that he must simplify and unify his life by making no further plans to keep in habitual touch with Margie on the principle that what they renounced, they recovered in God.

The monk forced himself into a heavy work schedule again, aided by growing fascination with his studies on the work of Camus and his translations of René Char's poems.

September

In early September, he began his private retreat prior to making his permanent commitment as a hermit. He went early into the woods each day to meditate, convinced it was God's will for him to live in solitude and to be faithful to the grace of solitude. Yet he could not sacrifice the belief that his vocation involved also a certain fidelity to his deep affection for Margie even though that appeared to be a pure contradiction. "I see that I am floundering around in the dark, and need to pray and meditate a great deal. And that it is true that this summer I have done some very foolish and dangerous things."

As his retreat continued, certain points became clear. First, he must be inflexible in making no attempt to arrange a future meeting with Margie, and he must not try to find ways of getting mail to and from her, particularly when this involved "outsmarting" the superiors. Second, he saw that if he had been fully aware of the meaning of his vows and commitment, he would never have let his love for Margie develop as it had in the beginning. The wrong steps, he concluded, began with his first love letter to her and the phone call on April 23 arranging to see her on April 26. He conjectured that if this were a "moral case" he would only be able to say that letter should not have been written, that call should not have been made. "They were, objectively at least, infidelities. And yet — I simply cannot say it without qualification. Was I being faithful in an obscure way to some other and more inscrutable call that was from God?"

In preparation for his commitment to solitude, and because he found himself still rationalizing and vacillating, Father Louis read back over his journal notes and correspondence. This review led him to conclude that they could have done one another terrible harm. He acknowledged that by the time their phone calls were discovered he had lost all will to resist if they had continued to see one another. The abbot's discovery of their attachment had helped resolve an impossible situation. "Dom James was more right than I was willing to admit, and after all pretty kind and not too unreasonable."

The hermit remained up late that night, until almost eleven, reflecting on the summer's experience, reading his notes and seeing himself in that experience as a man he did not fully recognize. However, the reality was there, "a deep reality and a disconcerting one."

Father Louis interrupted his retreat briefly on September 4 when he went down to the abbey to concelebrate with a group of fellow monks who were preparing to leave for a new foundation in Chile. He viewed this as a farewell to his brothers, but he entertained some hope that he might one day be sent to join them.

The days of his retreat were unforgettably bright and calm. He took long walks in the woods, morning and afternoon. After a final day of tormented struggle, he consented to "an inner letting go of any selfish hold on Margie or wrong need (I hope)."

Early Thursday morning, September 8, the monk walked down to the abbey where he read the short formula he had written:

> I Brother M. Louis Merton, solemnly professed monk of the Abbey of Our Lady of Gethsemani, having completed a year of trial in the solitary life hereby make my commitment to spend the rest of my life in solitude in so far as my health may permit.
>
> Made in the presence of Rt. Rev. Dom M. James Fox, Abbot of Gethsemani, September 8, 1966.[5]

The hermit described himself as "at peace" and he said Mass with great joy.

His mail brought the Bob Dylan records from Ed Rice. That evening, using a phonograph borrowed from the abbey for research purposes, he began playing the records. From the hermitage's open windows at dusk, "The Gates of Eden" and other Dylan songs sent brash new sounds into the silent forest. Such seeming incongruities amused the hermit. He found the songs fascinating as poetry, full of prophetic ardor and irony and power.

The weather turned much cooler in mid-September. Since chopping wood for his fireplace was now physically impossible, Father Louis asked about getting a heater and a tank of liquid gas for the hermitage.

Each evening he studied the Dylan records. The phonograph would soon have to be returned to the abbey and the recordings to Ed Rice at *Jubilee*. In addition he spent some time each day with the poems of Spaniard Miguel Hernández, whose "Lullaby of the Onion" he was translating.

His underlying preoccupation with Margie led to a preoccupation with universal aspects of human love. He took out the sketch for an essay entitled "Notes on Love and Need—April 1966" and wrote a new, much extended version which he titled "Love and Need—Is Love a Package or a Message?"

After a summer of living and observing his experience, meditating on it from every conceivable angle, this second attempt was far richer than the first, though not a finished essay by Merton's standards.

> In reality love is a positive force, a transcendent spiritual power. It is in fact the deepest creative power in human nature. Rooted in the biological riches of our inheritance love flowers spiritually as freedom and as a creature response to life in a perfect encounter with another person. It is a living appreciation of life as value and as gift. It responds to the full richness, the variety, the fecundity of living experience itself: it "knows" the inner mystery of life.

Although Merton was tormented by this period of profound emotional attachment, ultimately the experience confirmed for him what had before been intuitive conclusions. He could now know that his profoundest statements about love between two human beings held equally true about love between human and God, and that he himself had the capacity to love fully. Since he had never, during this experience, seriously questioned the validity or the priority of his vocation, the experience itself verified what he had intuited. His vocation consisted in the total gift of himself to God and through God to others. He now knew that he possessed an authentic potential for love and that his religious commitment was not the subtle disguise of an emotional cripple. This provided an inner liberation, which gave him a new sense of sureness, uncautiousness, defenselessness in his vocation and in the depths of himself. The change was not obvious. His problems were not solved at the level of day-to-day living, but the change could be perceived in a way that led Brother David Steindl-Rast of Mount Savior

Monastery later to describe Father Louis as at once so totally uninhibited and so perfectly disciplined.[6]

On September 17, Victor and Carolyn Hammer drove from Lexington for a visit even though Victor had suffered a slight heart attack only that morning. Victor talked of death. He gave Father Louis the impression that he was aware he might soon die and they might not see one another again. Afflicted by his friend's distress, the monk could find little to say, but after their departure he resolved to increase his prayers for Victor.

Merton returned to the hermitage with his mail. In it he found a letter from poet Cid Corman, the third from him in recent days. The first had been a lengthy and harsh rejection of what he considered the "violence of language" in *Raids on the Unspeakable*. The second had been an apology for the first. The third was an even more stinging denunciation. At first the monk simply disregarded it. Coming so soon after the visit with Victor, the whole matter seemed too petty. But he could never disregard criticism for long, and these reproaches from a fellow poet returned to his thoughts and finally made him doubt the value of his work and the purity of his literary motives, "without sadness or preoccupation." Merton concluded that he could "really get along without this nonsense. If I never wrote another book, I'd be happy enough." He felt that if he worked on creative writings privately, with no intention of publishing, that might be worthwhile "like weaving baskets and burning them as the earlier monks did."

Each morning the hermit set aside time to work on his booklet on Camus for the Seabury Reading Program's series Religious Dimensions in Literature.[7] And each day he attacked the stack of works waiting to be read. On September 20, he picked up a mimeograph of Jacques Maritain's conference to the Little Brothers of Jesus on their vocation. The conference, given in December 1964, absorbed Merton immediately and he wrote many pages of commentary in both English and French, finding it "the best thing I have ever seen on the 'apostolate of contemplatives.' "

October

In early October, Brother Martin de Porres came up to see about installing a gas heater for the hermitage. This was a hectic period of building for Gethsemani. The abbey church with its tall metallic spire and its imitative Gothic interior was being altered into a structure of far greater simplicity, felt to be more in harmony with the Trappist spirit. During this dismantling and rebuilding, conventual Mass was celebrated in a large room on the third floor of the cloister. A provisional A-frame structure had been set up just outside the enclosure for the celebration of private Masses and for public attendance at Mass.

On a Sunday afternoon walk in the cool autumnal sunlight of October 2, the monk paused on the forest path at the edge of his hill and looked down on the valley. The monastery without its ancient steeple was still a new sight, and it led him to reflect on recent events in the abbey. Later he wrote:

> I realized how much good there really is in this community—not only in so many individuals (this I have never doubted or questioned) but in the community itself as it is organized. There is real spiritual life, and hope, and charity, and love for God. An honest monastery, with all its shortcomings and failings—for some of these failings I am perhaps myself responsible, to some extent. But I count myself lucky to be here. There is really no other place in the Church now that I would rather be. I see so evidently that my hermitage is my true place in the Church. And I owe this to my community. Also, let's face it, to my abbot of whom I am so easily critical.

During this period of rehabilitation after the spiritual and emotional catharsis of the past months, the monk was profoundly nourished by his careful study of Karl Rahner's *The Dynamic Element in the Church*,[8] from which he copied out in longhand many quotations, such as "Ultimately, only one thing can give unity in the Church on the human level: the love which allows another to be different, even when it does not understand him." And, "A charisma always involves suffering. For it is painful to fulfill the task set by the charisma, the gift received and at the same time within the one body to endure the opposition of another's activity which may, in certain circumstances, be equally justified."

The monk notes that this was "pure gold—and especially important for *now*," and wondered if there were perhaps a hidden charismatic element in the "prophetic" work of Camus.

When Father Louis went down to the abbey to pick up his mail on October 4, one of the old monks whom he loved, Father Stephen Pitra, fell under the trees near the gatehouse. Monks in the immediate area, including Father Louis, knelt in the grass and prayed for him as he died. They carried the body into the abbey post office a few yards away, where Father Merton and Father Flavian sat beside it saying psalms until Father Stephen was taken up to the third-floor chapel. He was buried the next day "with much singing of birds on a bright morning."

The following few days were crowded for a solitary. On the evening of the sixth he received the long-awaited visit from Jacques Maritain, who was accompanied by Elizabeth Manual, the daughter of an old friend, Penn Jones, and John Howard Griffin. Merton described it as a wonderful visit. Jacques Maritain was making what he felt would be his last visit to the United States so that this was a "final meeting" for the two old friends. Early on the morning of the seventh, Father Louis came down from the hermitage and joined the visitors for breakfast at the abbey. Other old friends arrived: Father Stanley Murphy, C.S.B., from Canada and Dr. Dan Walsh. Father Louis took this sizeable group up to the hermitage where he built a roaring fire in the fireplace. Merton and Maritain sat on each side of the fire, warming their feet at the hearth, and simply basked in each other's presence. After serving his guests hot coffee in the two cups and half dozen glasses with which the hermitage was provided, the monk put on his glasses, leaned against his work table and read from his current work, experimental poems he called "Edifying Cables."[9]

Shortly before noon, Father Louis accompanied his visitors back down the hill to the provisional extern chapel where he celebrated Mass for them. As a special thoughtfulness to Maritain, whose knowledge of English was masterful but who in his great age became quickly fatigued following any language except French or Latin, the Mass was celebrated in Latin, in the old way, slowly and leisurely.

They returned to the guesthouse to take lunch with Father Abbot in the small private dining room. Over a meal of soup, salad, fish, cauliflower and potatoes, with white wine, they discussed vernacular translations. Maritain introduced the subject with an apologetic mention that some months before he had been talked into signing a petition asking that Latin be retained over the vernacular in some of the offices. He remarked that without much reflection he had been *"suffisament idiot"* to sign it, an act he now regretted. He had not objected to the vernacular in principle, he explained, but to the silliness of some of the translations, and he cited as an example the latest translation of the parable of the wise and foolish virgins. In French, traditionally, this has been rendered as *"les vierges sages et les vierges folles."*

"Now," he said to Father Louis, "can you imagine? — foolish virgins is translated as *'les vierges etourdies.'* "

Etourdi connotes something scatterbrained, dizzy, confused. Father Louis laughed and agreed that it was an unfortunate choice of words.

After lunch, Maritain began to wander toward a room at the opposite end of the hall. Father Louis turned him around and headed him in the right direction to go to his own room. Maritain pressed the palms of his hands against the sides of his head and mumbled apologetically to Merton, "Forgive me, Tom . . . *Je suis en peu etourdi aujourd'hui."* ("I'm a little confused today.") To which Merton spontaneously and sympathetically replied, "Yes, Jacques . . . like the virgins."

The monk told his guests good-bye and walked up the hill to the hermitage. Before he could settle in to work, he received a message that Dan Berrigan, who was not expected until the end of the week, had arrived.

The two friends concelebrated two Masses, one in the regular rite and the other, on October 13, with a new Mass Father Berrigan had brought with him. Father Louis contrasted these two Masses to the one he had celebrated for Maritain, which he described as "very sober, austere, solemn, intense," while those with Dan Berrigan were "very open, simple, even casual, but very moving and real." Although Father Merton retained a deep affection for the old ways of saying Mass, he wrote, "Somehow I think the new is really better."

Toward the end of the week, Brother Martin de Porres installed the new gas heater, which worked well but smelled bad. Father Louis preferred the wood fire, but he could no longer count on keeping a wood supply. As he stopped trying to chop wood, the bursitis subsided.

During the week of October 20, the monk's intestinal problems flared again and he was sent in to St. Anthony's Hospital in Louisville for stomach x-rays and other tests. He had a room in the new wing of the hospital, a room filled with sunlight all morning. But any trip to the hospital profoundly disturbed the monk, and this one was a trial because Margie and all the members of her nursing class returned to Louisville to take some exams. She came to the hospital twice for brief visits, enough to awaken the longing in Merton to see more of her. In the end he returned to the hermitage frustrated and disappointed. The attachment was less intense and he was freer. He had striven for precisely this, but it was painful to experience the change. He wanted to get out of this "senseless contradiction that has made everything go wacky for seven months," but it was disturbing to renounce the consolation of all contact with her.

The hermitage was particularly lonely that afternoon of October 27 when Father Louis returned to his solitude. That night, unable to sleep, he got up from his cot, dressed and walked in the cleared area in front of the hermitage in the chill clear evening under a full moon, "meditating, enjoying the quiet, the peace, the cool silence of the valley, and the freedom." He wrote that all he had ever sought was there. "How foolish not to be content with it—and let anything trouble it, without need."

The weekend of October 31 brought a momentous visit from Sidi Abdesalam of Algeria. Father Louis was at a complete loss for words to describe this extraordinary visitor whom the monk recognized as "a true man of God," and an authentic representative of the very best in Islam. Sidi Abdesalam was accompanied by Bernard Phillips of Temple University and a disciple and the latter's wife, who translated, as Sidi Abdesalam spoke only Arabic.

The visit strengthened Father Louis, who was holding a low opinion of himself at the moment, because the visitor expressed the highest regard for Merton and his work. The monk had sensed, before Sidi Abdesalam's arrival, that he came as a messenger from God. The visitor admitted feeling the same thing.

Sidi Abdesalam expressed his belief that the hermit was very close to mystical union and that the slightest thing could accomplish that union. This increased the monk's sense of unworthiness, and at the same time he experienced profound consolations at Mass that day. The long work of restructuring his life was greatly accelerated by Sidi's visit.

On the strength of his new direction, Father Louis sought to be absolutely honest with himself. In relation to Margie, he remarked on the ease with which human beings can deceive themselves in such a situation. He speculated that it might have been an attempt to escape the demands of his vocation, though certainly not a conscious attempt. Nevertheless it was a protestation of human love for a special covenant of loneliness and solitude, which were the very heart of his vocation. "I did not stand the test at all — but allowed the whole essence to be questioned and tried to change it. And could not see that I was doing this," he wrote. He believed that only God's grace had protected him from the worst errors and he saw it as God's grace that he was gradually getting back into his "right way."

A hard, steady rain began to fall in the early morning hours of October 31. Before dawn, Father Louis put on his raincoat and walked down the hillside to concelebrate at the abbey. When he returned to the hermitage, he carried a raincoat pocket full of eggs and prepared himself a much heartier breakfast than usual.

Toward noon the rain stopped. The hermit struck out for a long walk with an increased sense of freedom and discovery. He reflected again on the great help that had come to him from Sidi Abdesalam's presence and expressed determination "never to get caught again by a love affair and not to let this one flare up again. Only now do I begin to see the state of the ruins. What an embarrassing mess. And how completely stupid I have been." In view of all this he could not take seriously Sidi Abdesalam's belief that he was close to mystical union. A great purification was needed, and a spirit of penance, to which the monk now felt deeply inclined.

November

Within twenty-four hours the rains turned to a major snowstorm that lasted all night. Father Louis made his way down to the abbey to celebrate his three Masses early on All Soul's day. Others were no longer saying the three Masses, but Father Louis and a few older priests continued the custom.

In the early afternoon he walked out in the woods in the continuing storm and then returned to settle in for the afternoon, letting himself be enclosed by the snow and the silence in the warmth of his cabin.

He worked well on the Camus study and later cooked "a mess of rice" and found it good.

He resumed his work after supper, noting that everything was perfectly silent except for the wind howling in the dark and the noise of occasional boughs of evergreen breaking under the weight of the snow. He rejoiced in the hermitage, isolated by darkness and storm. "It is pure delight. I thank God for it. And again I am overcome with embarrassment to think how I have trifled with this grace."

He pondered the objective fact of his vow, which he saw as far more than a mere juridical obligation. "It has deep personal and spiritual roots. I cannot be true to myself if I am not true to so deep a commitment."

The next morning he was up at his accustomed hour long before dawn. As he finished his long period of private prayer and spiritual reading and meditation, first streaks of dawn were beginning to appear in the east. He surrendered all of his faculties to the sight, open to what it could tell him, thanking God that he was in this peace, solitude, joy; he was aware that everything depended on his fidelity to a vocation that he must stop trying to rationalize. "It is *there*. It is a root-fact of my existence."

This peace continued for the next few weeks as he plunged into a program to read and make notes on much of Faulkner's work. Merton followed his usual pattern of almost uncritical enthusiasm at the beginning, then a resifting of his opinions into a far more critical final evaluation. However, he admired Faulkner and filled pages of his workbooks with appreciative quotations and comments.

December

In early December, Merton's close friend W. H. (Ping) Ferry contacted the abbot to make arrangements for Joan Baez and Ira Sandperl of the Center for the Study of Nonviolence, to visit Gethsemani.

When the guests arrived and had been welcomed by Dom James, they spent the afternoon and evening with Father Louis. Despite heavy mists and cold, they took a long walk. Then Father Chrysogonus, the musicologist and composer, and Brother Richard Schmidlin joined them for a visit at the hermitage.

Father Louis built up the fire and they played one side of the singer's new record, *Noel*, sitting on the floor on the grey throw rugs around the fireplace. After Father Chrysogonus and Brother Richard left, Father Louis served some food. He was entranced by the sight of Joan Baez sitting on the rug in the firelight, eating goat-milk cheese, bread and honey and drinking tea. The three communicated easily, as though they were already old friends. He knew her music and she knew his books.

"Lovely," the monk wrote. "She is an indescribably sweet girl and I love her. I know she loves me, too. She said she had discovered prayer in reading my books and she and Ira seem to have read and liked my recent work. Great openness, warmth, support."

They discussed the work of Bob Dylan in whom the monk was deeply interested and about whom he intended writing an article. (The article never materialized.) In the particular joy of that meeting, in the hermitage, surrounded by falling rain, Merton confided to them the details of his falling in love with Margie and read some of the poems. They were so moved that Miss Baez was ready to drive at high speed to Cincinnati so Merton could see Margie when she got off from work at the hospital at 11:30 P.M. The plan was impossible, but the fact that she would offer it on such a night filled Merton with gratitude.

"A precious, authentic, human person," he noted. "The thing I sense most, for some reason, is a kind of mixture of frailty and indestructibility in her."

To prolong their time together as much as possible, the monk did ride in with them to the airport in Louisville, after arranging by phone for his friend Dr. Jack Ford to meet them at the airport and drive him back to the monastery.

As the year drew to a close, the monk's notebooks contained fewer and fewer references to Margie, and in those rare references that extended on into the first months of 1967, the tone is one of quiet sadness and acceptance of everything that occurred and of the inevitability of its conclusion.

"I have at least this solitude and this responsibility and this privileged silence. And a need to pray," he wrote on December 15.

Later, in February, he remarked on the great changes that had occurred since the previous September, when "everything was still charged with the power of our love. But I see it as folly and infidelity for me to try to keep it going even in my own heart now. I need simply to let go and move on. And that is what I am doing . . . and still retaining a warm and deep affection for her."

Toward the end of the year 1966, the monk spoke of securing the journal for twenty-five years after his death, but added that he had no intention of keeping the episode of his attachment to Margie entirely out of sight. "I have always wanted to be completely open, both about my mistakes and about my efforts to make sense out of my life." The situation with Margie, he felt, was an important part of the whole picture, "and shows my limitations as well as a side of me that is—well, it needs to be known, too, for it is part of me. My need for love, my inner division, the struggle in which solitude is at once a problem and a solution."

On this Christmas Eve of 1966, the hermit stayed in his cabin until time for him to walk down the hill in the "lovely, cold moonlight" to concelebrate midnight Mass in the monastery.

He celebrated Christmas day quietly with a long walk through the woods to visit his fellow hermit, Father Flavian Burns. When he returned to his cabin, he read the notes and Christmas cards he had received. He remarked that it had been a peaceful Christmas. When he arranged the Christmas mail he left out on his table a picture of Sy Freedgood's "pretty little daughter, Julia, looking sweetly at her horse."

1967

❖

Antipoem I

O the gentle fool
He fell in love
With the electric light
Do you not know, fool,
That love is dynamite?

Keep to what is yours
Do not interfere
With the established law

See the dizzy victims of romance
Unhappy moths!
Please observe
This ill-wondered troth.

All the authorities
In silence anywhere
Swear you only love your mind
If you marry a hot wire.

Obstinate fool
What a future we face
If one and all
Follow your theology

You owe the human race
An abject apology.
                    — Thomas Merton

January

Bells from the abbey, clanging out in the rain at 3:15 A.M. awakened Father Louis as the first sounds of the New Year.

He got out of his cot with the resolve to begin the new year by getting back to right order insofar as making his prayer and meditation what they should be. "Actually, my prayer life has not been *bad,* but not good either. Yesterday was a dark, rough, depressed day, but after a lot of anguish it ended in hope and comfort."

Doris Dana, friend and literary executor of Gabriela Mistral, arrived for a brief visit. She visited the abbey at the special request of Jacques Maritain, who had asked the abbot to allow Father Louis to baptize her. Since she was a skilled translator and an authority on South America, Merton found much to discuss with her. She brought him the *Missa Criolla,* which he enjoyed with reservations, and the *Missa Gitana,* which impressed him more.

The monk's hearing had always been a problem. Noises disturbed him and he had resorted to earplugs to sleep through the natural noises of the forest at night. In a note to Father John Eudes, Dr. Francis J. Paisel of Louisville wrote: "Father has tinnitus aurium due to degeneration of the acoustic nerve. He was started on Pavabid and we will recheck him in three months."[1]

With the return of cold weather, the hermit turned to Guardini's study of Pascal[2] whom he described as "my kind." The book so stimulated him that he had to stop frequently and walk around the hermitage in order to absorb the rush of ideas. "Yes, I know," he wrote, "the world is full of people who will want me to know that my reading of Pascal is vicious — like taking LSD. Fatal pessimism and all that. Jansenism."

On January 9, he received a letter from a former nun who hoped to return to her order, scolding him because she had read a review in *National Catholic Reporter* of *Raids on the Unspeakable* and *Conjectures of a Guilty Bystander,* and "telling me I was a naughty old world-hater and that the world was really lovely, how everyone really loved everyone else and all was Paradise in Texas."

Typically, even though Merton dismissed the letter as a naive and narcissistic document, he assumed that he was at fault for this kind of failure to understand his work.

Too loud, too sweeping, and excited, too preachy. When I criticize a *system,* they think I criticize them — and that is of course because they fully accept the system and identify themselves with it. All love and bliss! And they seem to have no idea that the affluence (which for them is the kingdom of God) has another side to it — the buried bodies of children in Vietnam and the Negro-Puerto Rican ghettos.

The monk spoke of such correspondents as "pious souls with their pretty myths about the world." Only the subject was different: "Instead of sweet Mary and Baby Jesus, it is now sweet sweet world of automation and jets and freeways — and tranquilizers, I guess also."

In the following week Merton received visits from new and old friends, all of them colleagues in one sense or another. Dr. James Holloway and Will Campbell drove in to see him in Campbell's farm truck. They had a lengthy conversation about Faulkner and his current unpopularity with the civil rights movement "and with everyone else on that issue; penalty for taking a unique personal position and not electing to run with the pack."

Later, Merton had the first of a number of visits from fellow artists in the Lexington area: the writer, translator and teacher Guy Davenport and the photographer Ralph Eugene Meatyard, who were accompanied by poet Jonathan Williams, then visiting in the area. All three men were relatively young, fully accomplished and functioning artists. They did not come to see Thomas Merton as the legend but to visit a colleague who did not have to play any "ideal-self" roles with them. As a result, the warmth between them was immediate and the visit a great joy to the monk. Since Father Louis's interest in photography was now fully developed, he was particularly moved by the work of Meatyard, who was doing "marvelous arresting visionary things. Most haunting and suggestive mythical photographs I ever saw."

At this time, Father Merton prepared and sent out a mimeographed letter to his friends — his way of keeping friends informed without writing individual letters.

Dear Friends,

There comes a time when it is no longer important to prove one's point, but simply to live, to surrender to God and to love ... More and more since living alone I have wanted to stop fighting and arguing and proclaiming and criticizing. I think the points on which protest has been demanded of me, and given by me are now well enough known. Obviously there may be other situations in the future. In a world like ours — a world of war, riot, murder, racism, tyranny and established banditry, one has to be able to stand up and say NO ... But I hope I will be able to give up controversy some day. Pray for me. When one gets older (Jan. 31 is my fifty-second birthday) one realizes the futility of a life wasted in argument when it should be given entirely to love.[3]

January 29 was the coldest morning of the year. The monk awakened in his hermitage with a severe cold. He remained in, close to the fire, and read in the stack of books on his desk. The weather turned abruptly warmer the next day and Father Louis could not wait to get out in it. After answering some letters, he raked and burned brush around the hermitage. Then he walked down to the abbey to fetch his gallon jug of water and his mail.

On his return he was astonished to see a truck parked beside the cabin, with a well rig on which was painted *Pee Wee McGruder, Shepherdsville, Kentucky.* Mr. McGruder had obviously come to dig a well for the hermitage, left his gear and gone away while Father Louis was at the abbey. "It stands there. I have seen nothing of any Pee Wee McGruder. Maybe tomorrow, my birthday, he'll start whaling and banging away at the rock on which this place sits."

Opening his mail he casually noted that one of the letters, from Father Bernard of Melleray Abbey in France, contained an invitation for Father Louis to come to France where Dom Columban Bissey, Abbot of Melleray, was to receive the Legion of Honor. Since Father Louis had been instrumental in getting Dom Columban the honor, his presence was requested at the ceremony.[4]

Father Abbot Fox, meanwhile, was also considering Father Bernard's request. Convinced that Father Louis's vocation demanded he remain where he was and free from distractions and travel, Father Abbot Fox was distressed by the invitation. Unaware that Father Bernard had not waited to get his permission before writing directly to Father Louis, Father Abbot Fox decided to draft a letter asking Father Bernard not to issue the invitation. He feared that once Father Louis heard of the invitation, he would be tempted to ask for what seemed a reasonable permission to attend the ceremony in France.

Once a precedent had been established, the abbot foresaw an avalanche of such invitations. That Father Louis knew of the invitation, however, became clear within a few hours. At that time Father Abbot Fox held in his hands the letter Father Bernard had written Father Louis, with Merton's typewritten note at the bottom of page one.

Dear Rev. Father:

What about it? How about a nice birthday present? You yourself often say it is good for monks of daughter house to visit motherhouse. —a summons from Father immediate surely can be obeyed virtuously and without scandal—*au contraire.*—To speak frankly: I need to see another monastery besides Gethsemani to get some perspective. I wonder if this is not God's will this time.

The decision is entirely yours and I do not seek to intrude my own will in any way whatever. But I think it would do me a pile of good, frankly.

Quid dicis?
In our Lord
/s/ b m louis

On January 31, 1967, his birthday, Father Louis read Father Abbot's reply:

My Dear Father Louis

Today—how thankful—how thankful you should be to God—
The anniversary of His bringing you into the world.

How much has He not done for you—from the very instant of your actual being, unto this day.

Especially—today—this latest unique gift of a hermitage—surrounded by all the milieu of silence, solitude, and seclusion.

Exempt from almost all possible temporal cares.

How grateful you should be.

Your gratitude to Him will be shown, not by words, but by corresponding with the silence—solitude—and seclusion He has provided for you.

"To whom much has been given—much will be expected"—as Saint Gregory says.

Take my poor, humble advice, dear Father Louis—do not go and spoil it all.

It is all so clear what God wills for you now.

One thing is certain—no matter how much your own self-will would like to start traveling, out of your hermitage—God does not will it.

God has given you this hermitage, not to quit it for a greater expansion of exterior activities.

But to remain in it, for a deepening of your interior activities—of recollection, meditation, prayer.

There is nothing that leads to more intimate union with God than what you have now . . .

But this is done—not by traveling around outside, but by going down deeper inside.

There is no other way.

This will cost—cost like fury.

That's why there are so few real contemplatives.

Why?

They do not want to pay the price . . .

. . . But there is no other way.

"I must decrease—" . . .

. . . All this exterior activity is not the work of the Holy Spirit—but of some other spirit.

That is the great temptation, especially of hermits—after a while in their cell—they long to get moving again—and always of course for reasons which they present to themselves, as most holy and necessary.

But take my advice—dear Father Louis, I—who have at heart, not merely your best Temporal interest—but your best Eternal interest i. e.—God's plan for you.

Resist this temptation to go traveling.

It will keep coming back—I'll guarantee that.

But resist it again. Each time you will be that much stronger.

As Saint Peter tells us—warns us:

"Diabolus tamquam leo, rugiens, circuit—
quaerens quem devorate
cui resistite—fortes in fide."

God will bless you for it.

Each victory will bring you deeper and deeper into that union with God alone—and Him only—which I know is your only goal in life.

I have already offered my Holy Mass for you and all your poor needs.

Your true friend in Him,
(unsigned)[5]

February

Although Dom James never actually refused permission, Father Louis had no difficulty seeing that the trip was out of the question and he felt more relieved than disappointed.

Though the weather remained unseasonably warm, the hermit still had not seen Pee Wee McGruder. On February 2, at dawn, the temperature was sixty, but lightning, thunder and rain came quickly. "Which means," the monk wrote, "this is another day when Pee Wee McGruder will not come and start digging my well."

By afternoon the warm rain had turned to sleet and snow and the temperature dropped. The change caught the hermit walking in the woods. He hurried back to the cabin, built a fire and made some hot tea. While drinking it he read a "good urbane book of Viscount Norwich on Athos."

On February 3, Merton had to go in to see Dr. Mitchell about the bursitis, and was disappointed to learn the doctor would have to operate at the end of the month. He went for lunch at the home of Mr. and Mrs. Frank O'Callaghan. To be in the home of a young, married Catholic couple was the rarest kind of experience for the monk, and it was somewhat a revelation for him to discuss, in the atmosphere of a home, the current issues in the church.

I realized how out of touch I am with what concerns married people trying to live in the city. Which is all right. I am precisely supposed to be out of touch with those particular problems. But I need to be more definite in my mind: not imagining I have to try to "keep up" with everything. Stay moderately informed—and go on quietly doing my job. People need me to be a contemplative and not a newspaper man.

On February 7, the Feast of St. Romauld, which was also Shrove Tuesday, the monk had finished reading through a manuscript on the Church from Rosemary Ruether. She had also written him a letter challenging his solitude. Although the monk felt she did not understand his solitude, he remarked that she was very Barthian, "which is why I trust her. There is a fundamental Christian honesty about her theology — its refusal to sweep evil under the rug and its 'no' to phony incarnationalism."

Thursday, Pee Wee McGruder came to begin drilling the well, but nothing important had happened as yet. At a depth of thirty feet he appeared to have hit a small cave.

Because of the Rosemary Ruether manuscript and correspondence, Father Louis began to reexamine the whole question of his conversion, and to distinguish in it the action of God's word and the attraction of a sacral and traditional and stable structure.

> This is important especially in my vocation. Now that the stability of these structures is really shaken — and I have done my own part in shaking them — I have to live really by God's word and a "true" Christian community and not cheat by relying on past cultural props which keep me comfortable. The whole church world argument on my work has been ambiguous because I bought the idea of a sacred and unworldly Christian culture and that up against the wicked world. Wicked had to be therefore modern, technological.

This division, he realized, was too easy.

> Anyway, it is much clearer now *where* fidelity is important. Fidelity to God in the Church — in a certain way *against* the Church as established and "worldly" and tied up with what is really dirty and demonic (Spellman's blessing of the Vietnam war as a "holy" war. That's what "holy" has come to mean all right.) To live in the Church with the realization that the Church itself is nevertheless full of sham and lies . . . This very fidelity means saying *No* to the lie that is in the Church. Not canonize its sinfulness.

Fully into Lent, Merton returned to the study of Camus. On February 19, he received a letter from Sidi Abdesalam asking where Merton was in his life, and hoping he was not bogged down in words his own or those of others. "What is best is not said."[6] The monk agreed, felt his meditation was still slack, but was wary of tightening on something merely imagined. "I do still wait, and listen, try for a more total awareness, more simple, and *no phony absorption.*"

His worst error at the moment, he believed, lay in his preoccupation, and a futile one. "The woods save me, and the sun and snow. Lovely songs of birds amid melting snow fields yesterday afternoon."

The time approached for the surgery and with it the ache in his elbow increased. The night before his departure for the hospital he sat in his cabin, full of pain, while rain and sleet poured down on his roof. He listened to the hiss of boiling water, then made some tea before going to bed. The sleet turned into snow.

By the next afternoon a wildly blowing snowstorm had developed. From the window of his hospital room, the monk watched it blow across the open spaces. He underwent surgery for the correction of the bursitis on Friday. "Not much to it," he wrote. "Woke up in the recovery room with children crying after tonsillectomies and young nurses gazing down at me like mothers."

By the evening of the February 23, he was able to take soup and a small portion of chicken. He remained in the hospital over the weekend, and on Sunday, February 26, he went to the O'Callaghans for the afternoon and dinner. He and Nancy O'Callaghan, who was eleven and a half, began to draw pictures for one another, using a pencil and pages from a tablet of eggshell drawing paper. Father Louis would attempt anything Nancy requested, and the afternoon produced drawings of a sleeping cat and a Shetland pony, along with a more ambitious one of a robust and gleeful lady riding a thin, distressed horse, with a caption from the horse's mouth saying, "She is heavy!"[7]

On Tuesday, he was released from the hospital. As he left, he cut the identification bracelet from his wrist.

FATHER M. LOUIS MERTON, OCSO
AGE 52 MRC #017619-8
DR. W. MITCHELL

He placed it into an envelope, addressed it to Nancy O'Callaghan, and mailed it as he had promised her during his Sunday visit.

March

The abbot insisted Father Louis spend the night in the infirmary but permitted him to return to the hermitage on Wednesday. Except for weariness, some soreness in the arm, "and a dirty bandage," he felt fairly well. By March 2, a week after he had entered the hospital, he was still unable to type comfortably, so he wrote his Camus review for *The Sewanee Review* in longhand.

On March 5 he received another letter from Rosemary Ruether, whom he described as the most fiercely anti-monastic person he knew. Her letters were an important stimulus to his thinking, however. She rejected the monastic idea as unchristian, and demonic, yet allowed some place for it in practice as a "service." Merton believed her antipathy sprang from the supposed claim which no monk in his right mind would make in that way, that the monk was the only true and radical Christian. This was a valid problem since historically the claim has been made and supported, with certain qualifications by the Church—that lay people were good Christians insofar as they adopted a quasi-monastic spirituality.

"On the other hand, Rosemary Ruether seems to be claiming quite aggressively that she represents the true radical Christianity and on the basis of her own authenticity, she is entitled to reject us—which makes the whole thing a little laughable."

Merton wondered if a special kind of hellishness went with the very claim to be a radical and perfect Christian. History was full of examples, including monastic ones, of intolerance, fanaticism, heresy, cruelty and love of power, all based on the claim to radical perfection. And he noted that the same thing was true in the secular sphere among political radicals.

The well-diggers had finally reached water down in the limestone.

The next morning at 7:30 the monk stopped work long enough to note a big glaring red sun in the east behind the bare trees even while a light rain fell on his roof. The squirrels were out, running in the grass around the cabin.

He walked down to the infirmary to change into secular clothes for his trip to Louisville to get his bandages changed.

Dr. Mitchell told him the stitches would come out in another week. The showers of that morning developed into a full storm by late afternoon when the monk was driven back to the abbey. He changed clothes again in the infirmary, remained for supper and afterward climbed the hill in the cold rain to his cabin.

During this period Father Louis was becoming deeply involved with the work of Louis Zukofsky. He had already reviewed some of the poet's work, and Zukofsky had responded with the offer to send some books. While in the hospital, the monk had "sent a scrawl . . . saying 'send books!' " Zukofsky had responded with a long letter full of family advice about bursitis. ". . . the way he and Celia fight back with aspirin and something else, some mystery from Squibb." The books arrived immediately and Merton fell into them with great enthusiasm, calling them perfect and the most moving modern poetry he had read. The ground of Zukofsky verse, Merton suggested, lay in the fact that the Zukofskys were a musical family. Their son Paul was a renowned violinist. It was not that Louis Zukofsky searched to make anything "musical" or "poetic"; "he just touches the words right and they give the right ringing tone."

> The fir trees grew round the nunnery,
> The grille gate almost as high as the firs.
> Two nuns, by day, passed in black, like
> Hooded cameras, as if photographing the world.[8]

During Holy Week, the monk received a whirlwind visit from his old and cherished friend Seymour (Sy) Freedgood, whom he had known since his Columbia days. On March 15, a Wednesday, Freedgood arrived late, after having wrecked a rented car driving from Louisville in the rain. When the monk went down to greet him the next morning, he found him bandaged and looking very bad. But Freedgood, as always, was irrepressibly inventive. He had drafted a letter ostensibly from Abbot Fox addressed to Mrs. Freedgood, explaining that he had got into a theological discussion with some of the monks and they had beaten him up, which accounted for his battered appearance. Dom James refused to sign such a falsehood, but Freedgood's powers of persuasion were strong, and finally the abbot went along with the joke.[9] Father Abbot Fox also recalled that he could not tell when Sy was joking and when he was not. Sy informed him that he was an intimate friend of the owner of Heinz 57 Varieties, and he would have his friend send the entire 57 to the abbey. Here, where the abbot was certain Sy was pulling his leg, he apparently was serious, because the 57 Varieties showed up at the abbey later.

Since Freedgood was still able to get around, he and Merton got permission to go to Lexington to visit ailing Victor Hammer. They found Victor seemingly improved and had lunch with Guy Davenport and Ralph Eugene Meatyard at the Imperial House. Meatyard showed Father Louis the photos he had made of the monk. "Strange and good," Merton commented.

In their discussions, Sy Freedgood urged Father Merton to get out and see things and meet people. Merton admitted Freedgood was probably right, but that he had neither reason nor motive for being insistent on this matter. The most he would want, in any case, would be the freedom to travel once in a while to very special places, "for instance a visit to Sidi Abdesalam, or to go to the Zen places in Japan."

After Freedgood's departure, Merton entered into the quiet of Holy Week, cherishing the cool, rainy spring nights and the intentness of the days. He reflected on Freedgood's advice, and he felt he was right in a way; it would be good to get out and speak to people and see with his own eyes and hear with his own ears. Still, it was better to do without it if it would mean getting caught up in "endless nonsense, lectures, conferences, dinners. Who needs all that? Rosemary Ruether seems to think that *that,* the 'world,' is what is real. The world of the body, the senses, etc. turns out after all to be the world of Muzak."

Merton believed that there in his woods he lived a more authentically bodily and even worldly, in the good sense, existence than those in the world. In view of that he was not at all certain that his desire to make occasional contacts outside the cloister was truly of the Spirit.

Yesterday afternoon, walking about in my own field and in the hollow where the deer sleep, and where a big covey of quails started up in front of me, I saw again how perfect a situation this is, how real, how

far beyond any need of comment or justification. All the noises of all
the programs, or of all the critics, do nothing to alter this.

On Holy Thursday, March 23, the hermit gave himself over completely
to the long quiet afternoon preceding the crucifixion. His activities were
simple, so as not to intrude on the watching and waiting. He burned brush
in the forest near the hermitage and noted again his love for the woods,
particularly those in the area of the cabin. He knew every tree, every animal,
every bird, and felt deeply related to all of them, a full member of the
forest community.

Easter came early that year, on March 26, but it was a warm summery
week, with redbuds beginning to bloom among the first faint clouds of green
in the woods, and birds gathering to sing. Easter Day, the monk said Mass
alone in the library chapel. Father Flavian walked over from his hermitage
to return Father Louis's Christmas visit. The two hermits talked for a while,
and then Merton took a walk in the sun.

The next morning, Pee Wee McGruder came and finished work on the
well. The hermit watched them weld the casing on the new grass and insert
it into the well.

His arm appeared to be doing less well than he expected. The pain
remained and he could do even less with it than before the operation. He
made an appointment to see Dr. Mitchell. The x-rays showed some calcium
remained in the joint. The doctor ordered him back on a regimen of rest
for the arm and heat treatments. "So back to the hot water bottles."

Since he had some hours to waste before catching his ride back to the
abbey, he called his friends. Dr. Wygal was too busy to join him for lunch.
Father John Loftus was out of town, and the line to the O'Callaghans was
tied up. Since he had some money, he went alone to The Old House, where
he had an omelet and got into a conversation with the head waiter, a black
man, who told him they were reading Bonhoeffer in their church study
group.

Afterward he bought some paperback books, science fiction, which he
had not read in twenty-five years, to see what was being done in that field.

He climbed the hill up to his hermitage with his packages, his arm aching
severely from the effort of getting the packages to the hermitage. At dawn
the next morning he looked over to see the familiar Pee Wee McGruder
well rig, and was shocked to find it gone. Now they had to put in "a pump
and a tank and a sink and a tap, and maybe I'll have water." The sooner
he could stop carrying gallon jugs from the monastery, the better it would
be for his bursitis.

April

Despite the pain in his left arm, he began the month of April with a
hard day's work on his Camus studies. However, with his inability to type

comfortably and the near-illegibility of his handwriting he felt stymied about getting promised work out. He thought about getting a tape recorder and reading from his handwriting, which even he could not always decipher, onto tape, hoping to find someone to type from the tape. This was a system he eventually adopted for much of his work.

That evening, he sat on the porch in the moonlight and meditated, listening to the trickle of water in the new well. He reflected in some detail about the approaching visit of attorney John Slate, who was to help him draw up a kind of literary will for the disposition of his literary estate when he died. His ideas were disorganized. "So much of the stuff left is junk — to be kept, perhaps, but *not* published."

Slate's visit brought a time of turmoil. The weather turned hot, up to eighty-four one day. Arrangements for the estate involved running back and forth to Louisville to see people at Bellarmine, where the bulk of it would be lodged. There the monk was recognized by too many people and even had to stop and sign autographs.

Eventually the estate arrangements were settled, after much discussion with everyone involved, in an acceptable way.

After John Slate's departure, the hermit sat alone again among the pines, relieved and quiet after all the talking. At such times, he recognized the strong hesychastic tendencies within himself. "I certainly have to recognize that when I am talking a lot and running around here and there I am simply *not myself;* and act and speak in a way which is not true to myself and to my inner grace."

His trouble lay in his feelings of guilt about his *hesychia.* And certainly that made sense, too, he said. A mere quietism was not good enough. What he needed was the inner freedom that was tranquil and unconcerned in everything, and he was making some progress in that direction. "Yet I am careless, untrue to myself, undisciplined, free with the wrong kind of freedom, talk too much, use bad language too much."

He valued silence and prayer, and then worried whether or not he ought also to conciliate the world with some of its own gestures. He had recently sent a statement on optional celibacy to a correspondent in St. Louis, and now he regretted having sent it, not that he had changed his mind on the subject. "Sure I think they (priests) ought to be able to marry if they want to. But why do *I* have to make noises about it? Probably means getting into a very stupid argument."

On the morning of April 8, the valley was as beautiful as it could be in spring. The redwoods were still blooming and now the dogwoods were flowering "like constellations in the green gloom of pines."

In his mail, he had a letter from Archbishop Dom Helder Camara, full of exhortations, praising Merton's book *Faith and Violence*, asking the monk to "encourage" Jacques Maritain not to be pessimistic and frightened, asking him to write to the pope, to write to Cardinal Maurice Roy. And couldn't organizers be persuaded to invite Merton to a second *Pacem in*

Terris Conference? On this latter, Father Louis noted that he had already been unofficially invited, or at least they had told him they wanted him to be present. But he had not even mentioned this to his abbot, not only because he was sure permission would be refused, but also because he was not at all sure he wanted to go.

> No, I would be scared of simply making a fool of myself and accomplishing nothing. There is no question that my 25 years in here have, for better or for worse, left me entirely outside the age of traveling by jet to conferences everywhere. I just do not belong any more to that world. Maybe I should belong in it—maybe I have made a mistake, I don't know. But the fact is that I belong in these woods.

Later that same day, he noted how confused he had been in past months. He felt it came from roots that had simply lain dormant since he entered the monastery.

> So, too, in my writing, my persistent desire to *be* somebody, which is really stupid. I know I don't really need it or want it, and yet I keep going after it. Not that I should stop writing or publishing but I should not let myself be flattered and cajoled into the business, letting myself be used, making statements and declarations, "being there," "appearing." I'm ashamed of myself.

At the root, though, he admitted an attraction for this kind of publicity. Or rather, he would like to be known, loved, admired, "and yet not in this cheap and silly way. But is there any other way? In any case, if I were more serious about remaining unknown I would not be so quick to accept what eventually shames me."

In his mood of self-reproach, the monk propped up on his table the photo of Suzuki standing amid laurels, which Winston King had brought him a few days before. He took comfort from the presence of that quiet, collected countenance. He wrote:

> All the old desires, the deep ones that are truly mine, come back now. Desire of silence, peace, depth, light. I see I have been foolish to let myself be so influenced by the current trends though they perhaps have their point. On the other hand, I know where my roots really are—in the mystical tradition, not in this active and anxious secular city business. Not that I don't have my obligation to society.

That evening on the porch, Father Louis sang the Alleluia and Introit (which would not be sung in community) for the following day's Mass. He read again in *The Book of the Poor in Spirit.*

He awakened the next morning, the Third Sunday after Easter, singing

Jubilate Deo, enthralled by "the lovely freshness of the morning." He listened to the resonant lowing of waking calves down at the barn. "Oh my sweet valley. Gregorian comes naturally out of this earth and this spring." He saw that the time had come to live without it, except such as he himself might sing in his hermitage.

During the following week, the monk learned that his old friend Dan Walsh was preparing for his ordination. Archbishop Floersh, on his own initiative, had decided this, got all the necessary dispensations and asked Walsh if he would not like to be ordained. The ordination had been scheduled for Pentecost Sunday at St. Thomas Seminary. "Dan is dazed. Everyone is astounded."

Father Louis's longtime friend and literary representative, Naomi Burton Stone, arrived on April 19 for business conferences. Father Merton remarked that they had two fine days, Wednesday and Thursday. He had arranged with Mrs. O'Callaghan to invite Father John Loftus and Ron Seitz for a picnic at the lake on Thursday. The monk enjoyed this kind of get-together, not only because it brought his friends together there in the Gethsemani woods, but also because he loved food and Mrs. O'Callaghan's sumptuous picnic menus were a great change from the monastic diet. Her list for this picnic included:

Broiled chicken with orange-jelly sauce
Cold pressed cucumbers with onion, parsley and dressing
Cajun stuffed eggs
Quiche Lorraine
Crackers and Camembert
French bread, butter
Olives and pickles
Cream cheese tarts
Fruits: apples, pears, grapes, oranges
Coffee, sugar, cream, wine

The group picnicked under a sun so bright Father Louis's nearly bald head got sunburned. He borrowed Mrs. Stone's Nikon camera, one of the few really fine cameras he had ever used, and took many photographs.

The monk acquired his tape recorder on April 22, and instead of taking his usual long walk, he experimented with the new machine to make certain he knew how to work it. "It is a very fine machine and I am absorbed by it and I am abashed by it. I take back some of the things I have said about technology."

Before going to bed, the monk stepped out on the porch and watched a full moon rise over the valley where everything was "cool, green and very clear." But he could not let the tape recorder alone and he stayed up late to work with it. He felt he was learning to use it and that it had real possibilities if handled with care.

One good thing about it: it may cool down my emphatic attitudes. I will do less underlining. Do not have to try to be so definite, so decisive. A kind of freedom can come from being nearly relaxed and cool and open. I have this interiorly, and can be this way when not speaking and not thinking. Important to be that way while speaking and thinking.

May

The monk's intestinal problems returned too frequently during those days, keeping him miserably uncomfortable along with his other discomforts. On May 2, he made his first visit with Dr. Tom Jerry Smith, an allergist with offices in St. Matthews. Since Merton had been referred to Dr. Smith by "a very able proctologist,"[10] Dr. Marvin Lucas, much of the actual physical examinations had been completed. Dr. Smith made only a cursory examination and went immediately into the matter of allergies. He found that Father Louis "relished a glass of beer occasionally which I had to prohibit." And he showed a sensitivity to beef and milk. Dr. Smith ordered a rigorous milk-free diet, which Merton found disconcerting because he could not always tell which foods contained milk. He avoided bread at breakfast the next morning, but tried some rye crackers, which he surmised and hoped might have no trace of milk in them.

His visit with Dr. Smith fascinated him, and on the fourth he left a note for Father John Eudes, the M.D. at the abbey:

Dr. Fr. Eudes:

Through the devious working of Providence I have now fallen into the hands of a new doctor who persecutes allergies with an entirely medieval frenzy. I am on a ruthless new diet, which works, it seems, if only because of the effect upon my awe-struck imagination. I have to see him again next Tuesday when all traces of any kind of milk or cow-like effluence have been purged from my humors. (I will need to go in at eight a.m. if possible.)

The purpose of my present note is this: since allergy suddenly appears to me in all its fantastic incoherence as an object of fruitful and amusing study, I would like to read up on the current myths about it. Can you give me any reading material, any articles from medical digests, or other stuff that comes your way. It occurs to me after reading that book of Foucault on madness that doctors are in reality creative artists with a remarkable flair for improvisation on people's backs, elbows, guts, etc. Since I am now a museum of such creative enterprises I feel that my self-understanding would be improved if, through appropriate reading, I could come to see myself as I am.

Seriously, I'd appreciate something to read that would let me in on

Guests at the hermitage include Jacques Maritain, Father Stanley Murphy, Penn Jones, and Father Dan Walsh.

Merton serves his guests, John Howard Griffin, Dan Walsh, and Jacques Maritain. (Phographed with camera on tripod, using a self-timer.)

Merton serves Mass, assisted by Brother Maurice Flood.

Self-portrait of the author, working in Merton's hermitage.

the mysterious thinking about allergies that is presently current.

in Jesu

/s/ br. m. louis[11]

That afternoon, Father Louis took a long walk in the woods and compared Ascension Day this year with that of last year. The weather was similar, bright and not too hot. Only a year ago, he had spent the afternoon with Margie Smith. Now it seemed almost unbelievable. "I kept thinking of it. But I don't regret that today was entirely different. Peace, silence, freedom of heart, no care, quiet joy. Last year there was joy and turbulence and trouble which turned into confusion and a deeply disturbed heart because I knew I was wrong and was going against everything I lived for." He looked up at the tall treetops and the high clouds and listened to the silence.

Father Louis finished reading *The Autobiography of Malcolm X* the afternoon of May 5. That evening, as he returned to his hermitage from the monastery, he found a dead mouse on his doorstep. He examined it to determine what had killed it but found no marks. "It was just dead."

Early the following morning, Merton was awakened by a severe colic, which mystified him because he had remained careful about his new diet. When he was somewhat recovered he opened Camus's *The Plague* to begin his work. He immediately began copying into his notebook, in French, the first passage he read.

On the morning of April 16th Dr. Bernard Rieux walked out of his office and almost stepped on a dead rat in the middle of the landing. He stepped around the beast without paying much attention and went down the stairs. But once in the street the thought came to him that this rat was not in its place.

The curious similarity between his experience of the night before and his reading in *The Plague* haunted the monk throughout the day.

His journal page is intercut with isolated sentences about it:

"A white-footed mouse."

"A dead mouse on the doorstep. Very curious."

" — On the morning of the 16th of April Dr. Bernard Rieux . . ."

He noted there was Bubonic Plague in Vietnam. He did not know how many cases there were, but presumed several. The moral plague, in any case, was serious enough. He said, as he had several times before, the *Mass in Time of Pestilence,* as one appropriate to our age.

Jim Holloway drove Daniel Berrigan from Berea for another brief visit. Father Louis remarked that Father Berrigan resembled a French worker-priest in a grey and black turtleneck sweater and black windbreaker, and saw it as a good uniform for a priest. Father Berrigan drove in with him for his appointment with Dr. Smith on the ninth. The monk was in the doctor's office almost two hours "getting needles stuck in me and contemplating a print of a fierce trotting race entitled 'A Race for Blood.' " Afterward, Dr. Smith drove Berrigan to the airport to catch a flight for New York.

When Father Louis walked into the gatehouse on his return, he saw Dan Walsh in black suit and Roman collar reading his breviary, having been ordained deacon the day before. His ordination to the priesthood was scheduled for Sunday, and Merton was to concelebrate.

With a sense of fatigue and relief the monk regained the quiet of his hermitage. For a long time, during the calm and cloudy dusk, he sat on his porch with field glasses and watched three does feeding in the horse pasture while dogs barked across the valley.

The hermit began a half-day retreat on the Vigil of Pentecost in preparation for his participation in Dan Walsh's ordination the next day. He described it as "a rather foul, murky, damp day," and his inner climate matched it. He experienced a deep need of conversion and penance, an almost engulfing sense of repentance, of having erred and of needing to get on the right path. He prayed for forgiveness, with "a real sense of being flawed and of needing immense help, pardon — to recover some capacity to love God."

At the same time, he sensed an atmosphere of decay in everything in society and in the Church. In that time of distress he saw little real substance "in the noisy agitations of progressives who claim to be renewing the Church and who are either riding some rather silly bandwagon or caught up in factional rivalries." As for the conservatives, "they are utterly depressing in their tenacious clinging to meaningless symbols of dead power. Their baroque inertia, their legalism. Disgust."

And the same aura of decay afflicted him in the "hippy movement," which was particularly distressing because of his genuine sympathy and real compassion for its good intentions. Not that he knew enough to judge, he said, but the whole matter appeared so phony, pointless and decadent now.

> A fake creativity, a half-dead freshness, kids who seem to be already senile in their tired bodies, their LSD trips — a sense of over-stimulation and of exhaustion. The gasping of a culture that is rotting in its own garbage — and yet has so many potentials. I know all of this is too pessimistic — I am trying to salvage something in myself by saying "I am not that at least." Yet I am part of it. And I must try to bring life back into it, along with the others.

In the early hours before dawn on May 14, Pentecost, Father Louis was up and at work researching a study he had been asked to do on Paul the Hermit. He reread St. Jerome's *Vita* while rain fell steadily in the forest around him. "A beautiful piece of writing with deep mystical and psychological implications — so that whether or not it is 'historical' is irrelevant."

Later in the morning, with Abbot James Fox and his brother, Bernard Fox, Father Louis drove through the rain to St. Thomas Seminary "way out in the fields somewhere toward Cincinnati, to participate in Dan Walsh's ordination."

They waited and had pictures taken. Finally the ceremonies began, and Father Merton felt the concelebration went well. "A great enthusiasm filled the large bright chapel crowded with people, friends and students of Dan, including some former monks with their wives."

Afterward, they drove to the Frank O'Callaghan home for the reception. Though the day remained grey and threatening, they were able to sit in the yard at metal tables. Father Louis drank champagne along with everyone else. The day's jubilance made him incautious and soon the champagne took effect. He became talkative, "going against all I had in mind earlier Pentecost morning," and then very sick. The following day, the O'Callaghans sent him the empty champagne bottle with one of the ordination invitations tied to its neck, and a written message: "In memory of Father Louis with apologies from Frank."[12]

On Tuesday, a bright and clear day, Father Louis concelebrated with Father Walsh at the monastery of Discalced Carmelite Nuns in Louisville. He described it as an intimate and quiet Mass, with the sisters visible in their choir behind the open grill and singing well. "It was deeply moving, a sense of light and joy and of spiritual *reality*, a most beautiful eucharist." Both priests felt purified and enlightened by this contact with the Carmelites. They had lunch with the Jack Fords, where Merton met some of the "very alert" young priests who taught philosophy at Bellarmine.

On Trinity Sunday, May 21, Father Louis noted that his breakfast reading, which was supposed to be light and informative, had turned to works on quantum physics. He found these studies dazzling.

Neils Bohr and Co. are definitely among my number one culture heroes. This magnificent instrument of thought they developed to understand what is happening in matter, what energy really is about—with their confrontation of the kind of thing Herakleitos was reaching for by intuition. It is terribly exciting, though I can't grasp any of it due to the fact that I have never had even high school physics, and the equations are just hieroglyphics that represent to me no known animal.

The visits to Dr. Smith continued. On May 26, Father Louis went to "this allergy man who looks like a musician," where more tests were made, and a special vaccine administered.

Merton reproached himself for his continued need to protest. He had accepted being a sponsor for the National Association for Pastoral Renewal, which was conducting a poll on clerical celibacy. "I ought to learn to just shut up and go about my business of thinking and breathing under the trees. But protest is a biological necessity. Part of the allergy, maybe."

After three quiet days, Will Campbell and Jim Holloway drove up the hill in Campbell's red fire truck and sat in the cool breeze talking. The monk, a member with them on the Committee of Southern Churchmen regarded them as brothers with whom he was perfectly comfortable and at ease. Will had brought his guitar and he sang some country music for the hermit, who remarked: "Curious. Such a different temper from the (Negro) blues."

The next morning Father Louis had a letter from Dom James in Europe. The apostolic delegate was inquiring about the monk's connections with the National Association for Pastoral Renewal, whose clerical celibacy poll had aroused Cardinal Spellman's disapproval. "I guess there is going to be a rumpus," Merton wrote. "Frankly I can't say I really care one way or the other. I sympathize with those priests who want to marry and continue as priests, and I think the continued opposition to them is going to mean trouble." His own feelings were ambivalent, and largely disinterested. In the long run, he was not sure if a married secular clergy really would solve anything for the Church, or for the clergy. "My own feeling is that it does not matter—much, and I am not deeply enough involved in the issue myself to get into a fight about it. I am an adviser of the National Association for Pastoral Renewal—that is a name on a list ... That is the extent of it."

June

Tuesday, June 6, brought a new experience and a change of pace into his existence.

Frank and Tommie O'Callaghan, their children, and some other friends from Louisville came out for a picnic that day. The monk found it pleasant but bewildering,

> all this movement and brightness and multiplicity—fishing, pogo sticks, soft ball, a frisbee, other games the names of which I never knew—children filling my hands with rubber crabs and flies they made in school. Questions coming and going: "Now I'm going to sit here next to you. Keep my place for me, don't let anybody take it ..."

After their departure, the monk walked back toward the abbey in the new silence with one of their souvenirs in his hand. He made his way meditatively into the library, ascertained no one was looking, and placed a huge black rubber fly on the open dictionary.

Gradually, running water was arranged for the hermitage. In early June, three months after the well was completed, a pump was installed, and also a small hot water heater with some temporary faucets, so Father Louis could wash his dishes in a bucket. This was a great help.

The hot weather had arrived by mid-June, with the temperature between ninety and one hundred in the afternoons. He spent more time in the woods, meditating and reading under the trees where it was slightly cooler.

After frequent trips to see the doctor in Louisville, the allergy shots seemed to be working, and Father Louis looked forward to a less interrupted solitude. He found a place near the doctor's office in St. Matthews that sold Kosher foods, so he laid in a supply of kasha and potato pancakes.

July

On July 4, a bright and cool morning, he heard a truck rumbling up through the field. He looked out to see his new bookcases swaying above the cab, which also meant that the sink and kitchen cabinet were arriving. The kitchen was quickly installed, the water connected and Father Louis gave the whole place a good cleaning, "gathering the books that were piled all over chairs and everywhere. The new furniture smells marvelously of fresh cedar and the place is really transformed by it. At last the kitchen is a real kitchen and I don't have to wash dishes in a bucket on the floor."

To celebrate, he prepared a supper of chop suey and rice. Afterward he walked "in the clear cool evening utterly at peace and happy with the cottage." He stayed up late "just walking around smelling the good smell of the cedar wood, looking at the new look of the rooms, and loving the place to be as clean as it now (for once) is."

Now that it was no longer necessary for him to make frequent trips down to the abbey to fetch his water, Father Louis asked for and received permission to have an altar and say Mass in the hermitage. He was driven to Athertonville to see Buck Murfield, the cabinet-maker, about building an altar as quickly as possible. He hoped to have it in time to say his first Mass in the hermitage on July 16, Feast of Our Lady of Carmel, patronal feast of the hermitage.

Two days later, the news that he had been expecting and dreading came: Victor Hammer was in the hospital in Lexington, partially paralyzed and in an oxygen tent, in critical condition. The monk's attention focused on his old friend. He began to fast, and while rain fell hard outside, offered Mass for Victor, saying the collect for the dying.

It was a difficult fast. Without coffee in the morning Father Louis sank into a torpor. He noted later in the week that he read with indifference and incomprehension about starvation in Camus' articles of 1939. The following morning, he lightened the fast with some coffee and eggs for breakfast. He reread the same passages from Camus with understanding and indignation. "So the luxury of being articulate depends on a certain detachment, disinvolvement. Is it better to participate in the stupor of hunger and having nothing to say? Both are necessary: hunger and silence, nourishment and speech."

He resumed his fast, but this time drank some tea in the mornings, "which makes all the difference insofar as keeping one's *mind* alive goes."

On Monday morning, July 10, the rain turned into a deluge. As the light began to grow, the monk looked out and saw that the bottom fields had become flooded. He walked out during a lull and saw through the trees the rushing flood water, and "an old tire riding up very fast on muddy waves." He was afraid Buck Murfield might be flooded out and would have to stop work on the altar. The next morning he arranged a ride to Athertonville, where the flooding had been bad. Some of the houses still had water up to the porches. "But Buck and his wife were planing away in their shop, which was full of the sweet smell of cedar."

On his return to the abbey, he learned that Victor Hammer had died the day before, while Merton was rained in at the hermitage. He said Mass for Victor and noted his death as "a great loss."

Again, he reproached himself for seeing too many people. He felt that to have to spend an afternoon with a visitor twice a week was far too much, that even once a week would be too much. He would like to reduce visits to one or two a month. He had no reticence about visits that were in line with his work, but just visiting and socializing, no matter how pleasant and edifying, troubled him afterward. Also, he was involved in projects that might constitute "cheating" on his solitary vocation.

> For instance—the collection at Bellarmine, the collection of Sister Therese—and all the business of filing and cataloguing every little slip of paper I ever wrote on. What a comedy. But I like it and cooperate whole-heartedly because I imagine it is for real. That I will last. That I will be a person studied and commented on ... This is a problem.

Another problem lay in his difficulty in saying no to almost any request that sounded reasonable. With the exceptions of invitations for Father Louis to go traveling to meetings, Abbot Fox usually left decisions about work or visits to the hermit. For example, in a note dated July 13, Abbot Fox told Father Louis of a request he had received from a Catholic editor who wanted to visit Merton for an interview.

> Since I didn't know him from Adam, nor could I grasp what he really wanted over the phone ... I told him to write me all about it. Then we would have something in black and white that I could turn over to you and you could evaluate it from all angles and judge it as you saw fit.
>
> So the letter came here with this copy of a magazine and you decide what you want to do.
>
> Do you want him to come down for an interview or what answer shall we give him?
>
> I'm utterly neutral about the whole affair. Let me know sometime what to answer him.[13]

Saturday, July 15, Father Louis went to Athertonville in the early afternoon to pick up the altar, "sweet smelling, in Murfield's dark shop." The day was bright and cool, the air washed clean. He set up the plain, cedar altar in the hermitage, with icons over it.

The next morning at 4:30, surrounded by the fragrance of candles and cedar and the damp odors of the forest, Father celebrated his first Mass alone in the hermitage. He said it slowly chanting the Gregorian Kyrie, Gloria and other parts. "It was a beautiful Mass and now I see that having the altar here is a great step forward," he wrote.

Saying Mass in the hermitage and having dinner there changed the shape of the day. Without the need to go down to the abbey, he felt a greater sense of undisturbed time. "The best Sunday I can remember in a very long time. The morning was perfect."

Father Louis began getting reports that someone was impersonating him. Frank Sheed (of Sheed and Ward), in London, had received a phone call from a man in Cleveland who claimed to be Thomas Merton. Since Sheed knew Father Louis's voice, he was not taken in. "Also, someone has been collecting funds, pretending to be Thomas Merton," Father Louis wrote in his summer letter to his friends. He warned his friends to be wary, and if possible to send any information that could help identify the person or persons involved in these schemes. The mystery was never solved.

In late July, the Abbot General of the Order, Dom Ignace Gillet, arrived for a visitation. Before dawn on the morning of the July 27, Father Louis was awakened by a violent storm with "continual lightning, and as I was putting on my shoes a terrific thwack of lightning striking in the woods near my cottage. I jumped. After Lauds (which I recited with more devotion than usual!) the storms cleared a bit."

At midmorning, when Father Merton was saying the Little Hours, he heard the distant clangor of bells ringing for a death in the monastery. It was Father Nicholas Caron, a monk from Holy Spirit Abbey in Conyers, Georgia, the translator at the visitation. He had suffered a heart attack while translating for Dom Gillet and died an hour afterward.

Father Louis was pressed into service, replacing Father Nicholas as translator for the remainder of the visitation. This reentry into official community life produced some discomfort for Father Louis, who had been out of community almost two years, long enough to have lost touch. He felt ill at ease going back each evening into the community chapter.

August

A part of Merton's uneasiness sprang from an episode that once again involved an invitation to travel, one about which he was not given all the particulars. This concerned a lengthy correspondence between Abbot Fox and various officials about a meeting with Cardinal Koenig of Austria who was to make a visit to the United States for conferences at Fairfield University in Connecticut dealing with nonbelievers and the church. The sponsors of the meetings had already lined up such eminent men as Norman Cousins, Walter Kaufman and Charles Frankel and hoped that the abbot would see the program as sufficiently important to grant exceptional permission for Merton to participate.

Father Abbot Fox in careful letters to the sponsors, explained why any exceptional permission in this case, important as the meeting was, would establish a precedent that would simply make it all the more difficult to refuse similar future invitations. In a letter to Cardinal Koenig, dated August 7, 1967, Abbot Fox wrote:

> We understand that efforts will be made in order to pressurize permission for this trip, that you will be asked to write to Father Louis personally.
>
> Dear Cardinal, we are most willing to do everything possible within the spirit of our order and community to make your visit to the United States profitable.

As an alternative to allowing Father Louis to attend the meeting, the abbot suggested, "nothing would give us greater pleasure, if you could fit it into your schedule, to come here to Gethsemani to visit with us and with Father Louis or any other monk here in the monastery." He pointed out the trip would take only about an hour and a half by plane, and that Cardinal Koenig could leave New York in the morning, spend the day at Gethsemani and be back in New York that evening. The abbot offered to pay all of the expenses for such a trip.[14]

In a letter of the same date to Rev. Richard W. Rousseau, S.J., of Fairfield University, the abbot, recognizing the value and importance of the meeting, explained his position in great detail.

> You can well imagine that we receive many letters requesting that certain members of our community—such as Father Louis—be allowed to leave the monastic solitude in order to participate in panels, forums, symposiums, workshops and so forth . . .
>
> . . . Your particular project, as I understand it is certainly most worthy—"In Se."
>
> But if God has called us to a cloistered life—of silence, solitude and seclusion, with Him—why try to pull any of us out? And *a fortiori* in the case of Father Louis—who is going beyond the ordinary silence and solitude and is trying to live an hermetical form of life here in the woods of our property.
>
> We are not indifferent or callous to the present great problems which confront the People of God—Holy Mother Church. On the contrary, we are very sensitive to their gravity.
>
> But cannot there be just a few dear Father—at least a "hand full"

who will be allowed to try to be the most united to God—alone with the Alone—in order to bring down graces for the human family?

. . . I have sought advice from other distinguished persons and they have all agreed that we should maintain our policy of silence, solitude and seclusion for all of our monks.

As good Father Barnabas Ahern, C.P., said to me: "Father Abbot— believe it or not—Father Louis does more for the People of God by remaining in the monastery—than by leaving it, for these meetings."

Once again, Abbot Fox assured Father Rousseau that if any of the members of his "gathering" wished to come to Gethsemani to confer with Father Louis, they would be welcomed and every facility for conversation would be arranged.

Such incidents led to uneasiness on Father Louis's part. He knew that he had been invited to attend the meeting with Cardinal Koenig, and he did not really want to go. "For my own part I do not need to be present at a meeting with Cardinal Koenig and it is just as well that I don't get involved in something that might lead to a 'career' of sorts, so honestly I am not sorry about that."

This sort of thing frequently led people to believe that Father Louis and Abbot Fox were constantly at loggerheads with one another. In the irritation of these incidents, Father Louis let his feelings flow over into almost everything he read or wrote, he himself being the first to recognize that in this overflow he was frequently childish and unjust.

This incident colored his view of having to translate for Dom Gillet, of having to return to chapter after such a long absence from the community and even in his impatience with things that usually aroused his sympathy.

Read a hippy underground paper from Cleveland and felt the same about that. It is silly. Then I read a little poetry magazine. The same. Do I now have to think there is something the matter? This does not follow. I will no doubt have to go to Chapter for a few days and do my silly bit. But I don't have to read hippy newspapers and poetry magazines that still take themselves seriously or anything else of that kind.

After a night's sleep, he was feeling better the next day. "Fortunately I have got over that particular bout of nonsense."

He added, "I am undoubtedly feeling the effects of 25-26 years of total institution, in which I have been freer than most but in which because of my insecurity I tend to bog down in self pity and self defeat."

These periods of dissonance were almost inevitably initiated by the unexpected intrusion into his life of some outside force—an invitation that in some way appealed to him and that got turned down by superiors even before he had arrived at the point where he would have turned it down himself; or the unexpected appearance of someone he was asked to see even when he might very much want to see that person himself.

He struggled against his resentments, but they had to work themselves out and they were always followed by a period of contentment that was deeper than usual if only by contrast.

Part of Father Abbot Fox's apparent over-reaction to such innocent invitations—the one regarding Cardinal Koenig, for example, or the one requesting Father Merton's presence in France—sprang from his having lived through such anguish in the past with Father Louis, and his dread of anything that might unleash this kind of interior conflict again.

During the early morning hours of August 9, lightning hit the utility pole next to the hermitage and blew out some of the lights. Father Louis had already finished Mass and he read with a kerosene lamp. He remarked that he could have said Mass by candlelight, and in fact did this after the *Sanctus.*

The church at the monastery was almost finished. Father Louis was pleased with the alterations but was glad that it was basically the same "after all those years of sweat and patience and exaltation in the old one. So many memories of the old church—the energy and agony I had to put into just getting through some of the ceremonies—and yet I remember it all with a kind of joy, because of the graces, especially of the first days here. And being hebdomadary, singing the Mass was a joy too, though I was often so painfully nervous about it."

The last two weeks of August were difficult. He became ill with the flu and a general weakness. On August 28 he sat on his cot drinking Linden tea, which he described as the best flu treatment for him.

"This sickness has taught me something: first perhaps that I am too obsessed with reading and work—and I know the pressure of letter writing is too heavy." Saying Mass that morning he realized that some of the best of the day was lost "with my nose in a book."

He spoke of August 30 as a "serious day." Work on the church was finished. The noises of machines had been silenced. The woods were once again quiet. It was a day to sit down and take stock, and come to decisions. He was simply overburdened by the kind of merciless demands that so often come from religious people with a good cause.

I am more and more oppressed by the mail that comes in. So much of it is fakery and/or manipulation. People trying to get something out of me or use me for something, even with the most "religious" of intentions: so much of the mail shows the kind of moral brutality that is everywhere latent ... In a word I am bombarded by bakers, fakers, con men, business men, and operators and good-enough people who want to talk me into something I am absolutely not interested in.

He concluded that he was thoroughly sick of all of it, and that he was not going to continue "playing around in the general games."

He reflected on Dan Walsh's report about the theology conferences in Toronto in which some bishops had been hooted for their talks. "There is too much spite, envy, pettiness, savagery and again too much of a brutal and arrogant spirit in this so-called Catholic renewal."

He was nauseated by the bad odor of the war, the cruelty, the intellectual confusion. "I prefer the air of the woods."

He felt with the greatest seriousness that the world was in for difficult times, but that his role was no longer to talk about it.

I have said what I knew how to say, and it wasn't much. Now I see no point in trying to cope with piles of mixed-up and unconnected information and opinions or to keep up with what "everybody is thinking." Better to stay out of it, not be used, do what I am really supposed to do and live the life that has been given me to live. That is the important thing—if I can do it.

September

The quiet days continued into September. The monk put his work aside and spent most of the daylight hours in the forest praying. With the exception of some necessary letters, which he wrote and took down to the abbey to mail, and the need to get the heel fixed on his right shoe, he avoided all contacts.

He fasted, finding this helpful, not so much so because of its penitential note but because it involved a change of tempo and perspective. "Instead of dinner—being out in the woods, seeing everything in the light and silence of noon—the unusual quiet—all machines stopped." He walked barefoot in a mossy spot under the oaks and pines and began to look through a new book that had come to him in the mail, a review copy of Peter Nabokov's *Two Leggings*. The book intrigued him because it described a Crow Indian, his fasts and his efforts to acquire vision.

On September 3, the new church was consecrated. Since Father Louis had been involved in its transformation, he experienced a sense of relief in its accomplishment. He prayed deeply over the problems of the abbey and the monks. On the seventh, Abbot Fox informed him he had reached a decision to resign and live in a hermitage in Edelin's Farm—some miles from the monastery proper.

"I was surprised," Father Louis noted, "and I respect him for the decision. In fact I envy him the little place Brother Clement has planned for him, out on a high spur—and it will be much more solitary there than here. Solitude may be much more rare here in ten years time—if I am still alive."

Almost simultaneously he received a new series of blows. First the news of Ad Reinhardt's death. Then came word from Ed Rice that *Jubilee* had collapsed. He not only worried about his friend, but he was disturbed at this evidence that a magazine of the high quality of *Jubilee* could not survive in today's world. Since he had often written for *Jubilee,* and since he had been so close to both of its founders, Robert Lax and Ed Rice, the collapse of the magazine was almost like a personal failure, a personal rejection.

After his meditation, "a good one in an anguished way," he went to the Bible needing comfort. He read Isaiah 44: 21 and 22:

> Remember these things, Jacob
> and that you are my servant, Israel.
> I have formed you, you are my servant;
> Israel, I will not forget you.
> I have dispelled your faults like a cloud,
> your sins like a mist.
> Come back to me, for I have redeemed you.

Father Louis said no reading "could have been better, *Deo gratias.*"

By September 11, Father Louis felt that although the preceding days had been extremely painful. "I can see the whole thing has been good — the kind of good anguish that squeezes and sweats a lot of nonsense out of you." That evening, after a walk in the forest, he began to work again, stopping long enough to prepare a supper of rice, chop suey and Chinese tea.

On September 22 he felt well recovered. He set out for a long walk, picking up his mail as he passed the abbey. It was a brilliant, warm early fall day. The trees had not begun to change and the grass was still green. The lake at St. Bernard's field was blue and calm. He walked there fasting, and at noon he opened his mail to learn that his attorney, John Slate, had died of a heart attack on the nineteenth in St. Francis Hospital in Roslyn, L.I. The monk walked in the sun, trying to comprehend it. "I know I too must go soon, and must get things in order. Making a will is not enough, and getting manuscripts in order is not enough."

He was working into a new regimen, which he found most helpful. He took coffee in the morning when he awakened, fasted through the day, avoided lunch, and had his meal about 4:30 in the afternoon. He said that replacing the noon meal with a meditation in the fields was the greatest help.

After talking with James Laughlin on the telephone on Sunday, Father Louis decided to go ahead with his attempts to set up a trust for his writings in spite of John Slate's death. Laughlin suggested getting an attorney from the Louisville area.

The monk thought of the Louisville attorney John Ford. On Wednesday September 27, Mrs. Pat Oliver and Martha Schumann, who were handling the Merton Room at Bellarmine drove out to go over some papers. They sat in the car during the first downpour of a long rain. Father Louis had just received a shipment of his photographs from Gregory Griffin, whom he had asked to develop and print his negatives, and he remarked that the women got away with some of them before he had had a chance to study them.

With John Slate's death, and Father Louis's decision to go ahead with the trust, the Merton collection at Bellarmine was much on his mind. He began to read G. Bachelard's *La Poètique de l'espace.* Bachelard's study of houses, rooms, "demeures" opened up a whole field of speculation for the monk.

In the light of this, he concluded the hermitage was right for him.

But the *Merton Room* — to which I have a silver key, and where I never go, but where the public goes — where strangers are and will be.
A bloody cuckoo's nest.

He saw it as an image of his own lifelong homelessness and rootlessness.

A place where I store away endless papers, in which a paper self builds its nest to be visited by strangers in a strange kind of unreal intimacy.
The anxiety I have felt lately is due probably to the surfacing awareness that all this is futile — a non-survival. A last despairing childish effort at love for some unknown people in some unknown future.

The rain continued steadily through the next day, "quiet and lonely in the hermitage with rain batting down interminably and a fire on the hearth."

He spent a good part of that day trying to get things in order, burning papers in the fireplace. He decided that he must get a better system to combat the accumulation of paper. Perhaps he should throw it away at the monastery before bringing it up to the hermitage. Perhaps he should simply stop answering letters. "Yet as soon as you say that something more heartbreaking than ever comes in and you have to acknowledge it — or some business presents itself and I am sold on it."

His thoughts turned back to speculating about the Merton Room once more:

. . . ambiguity of an open door that is closed. Of a cell where I don't really live, where my papers live. Where my papers are more than I am. I myself am open and closed. When I reveal most I hide most. There is still something I have not said: but what it is I don't know, and maybe I have to say it by non-saying. Wordplay won't do it. *The Geography of Lograire.* Writing this is most fun for me now, because in it I think I have finally got away from self-consciousness and introversion. It may be my final liberation from all diaries. Maybe that is my one remaining task.

October

After the brief absence from his work, enthusiasm for his work returned, and in the first week of October he wrote on *Two Leggings* and finished the preface to the Japanese translation of *The New Man*. He felt it was perhaps unreasonable to undertake so much, "but each is also an act of love and communion — Indians — Japanese — Puerto Ricans."

During the following week, Dr. Rosemary Haughton visited the abbey between lectures in Minneapolis and Chicago. She impressed Father Louis as a quiet and intelligent woman, concerned about true contemplative life. She impressed him also as being the first theologian he had ever met who was six months pregnant. He photographed her in a long black cloak with her hair blowing in the wind as she sat on the concrete dam of Dom Frederick's Lake.

He made his decision to seek the help of John Ford in Louisville in setting up the Merton Legacy Trust, which had dragged along almost three years without being put in final order. He decided that the trustees should be his friends and longtime colleagues in the publishing field, Naomi Burton Stone and James Laughlin, and Tommie O'Callaghan, to have someone in the Louisville area. On October 17 he wrote asking Mrs. O'Callaghan to be a trustee:

> Dear Tommie
>   ... The responsibilities of the trust will be simply to take care of the publication of unpublished materials and to protect the literary estate, the drawings and so on. The estate will be owner of all the materials, including those held in deposit under the custody of places like Bellarmine. And the money will go to the abbey. I hope you can be on this team. Naturally all the publication work will be handled by J. and Naomi.[15]

On October 27, Doris Dana, friend and literary executor of Gabriela Mistral, arrived for a second visit. They walked in an empty cornfield on a cold and windy afternoon, talking of Jacques Maritain, Kolbsheim, Spain, Gabriela Mistral. The next day they drove to Lexington to visit with Carolyn Hammer and then went to John Jacob Niles's farm for lunch and to hear his musical settings of three of Father Louis's poems.

The monk was entranced by the day, by the appearance of the Niles home in the country, by the homemade cider and the ballads John Jacob Niles sang and played on the lute. As they finished lunch, the soprano Jacqueline Roberts, and the pianist Janelle Pope, arrived and joined them for coffee. Then they listened to the songs. Niles had set *Messenger, Carol,* and *Responsary* (1948) and was working on *Evening*. To hear poems that had come from his own creative energies, set to music that was deeply felt by the composer, was an intense experience for Father Merton, and, he felt, for Doris Dana also. He was tremendously moved by the artists. "I was grateful to them for their own response to the music and the poems. It was an afternoon I enjoyed, and I burst into tears at Jackie's singing. And John said . . . that my poetry moved him to tears. So we were all ready to weep and in fact weeping."

Sometime during that same day Father Louis took the time to send this brief handwritten note to Father John Eudes. "If you have not done so, I strongly recommend you take a look at the *American Heritage* for October 1966 now on display in the library."[16]

Father John Eudes Bamberger followed Father Louis' advice and went to the library where he found that the front cover of that issue of *American Heritage* contained a painting dated 1848 by a William Rimmer. The painting showed a sailing vessel in the background and a group of men in a rowboat in rough seas in the middle-ground and a placid lady with her head held up clinging to an oar and floating in the water in the foreground. The painting is entitled "Mrs. Bamberger comes to America."

November

John Ford worked quickly to draw up the trust indentures. By November 3, Father Louis was able to write the potential trustees that everything had been cleared with the abbot about his new will. He hoped to set up a meeting on November 14 for signing the trust agreement.

On Saturday, November 11, Father Louis hurried through the rain to the abbey for an afternoon concelebration and Brother Richard Schmidlin's profession. "At the end we all recessed singing 'The Church's One Foundation' which reminded me of dreary evening chapel at Oakham thirty-five years ago. Re-newal? For me that is a return to a really dead past. Victorian England."

The next day, Sunday, Father Louis assumed that Naomi Burton Stone had arrived at the abbey and they could soon complete the trust arrangements, which had turned out to be much more elaborate than he had anticipated.

As usual, I began to have doubts about it when it was too late. But I think I have done right, though this recourse to law is neither "monastic" nor "anarchic." Still, I think it would be silly to leave a pile of paper that I have covered with ink merely to rot or get lost in the monastic library. What is left over after my death (and there is bound to be plenty) might as well get published. I have no guarantee of living many more years. Perhaps five, perhaps ten.

The final signing of the trust agreement, which took place on November 14 when Father Louis and Naomi Burton Stone went to Tommie O'Callaghan's home in Louisville, was a great relief to the monk. "Having put all my writings in the hands of this Trust, I am much less concerned about getting anything 'done'—still less about getting it published, obviously! I feel much freer and ready to forget all that, and make more out of solitude."

In the quietness of the remainder of November, Father Louis began to put into action a project that was to become one of his delights—the publication of four issues of a literary magazine to be called *Monks Pond.* He began to mail out notices of this and requests for photos, articles, poems and artwork to people who might be interested in contributing.

Toward the end of November, he remarked on one of the refectory readings at the abbey. Brother Richard was reading from a text of Hugo Rahner on *Man at Play.* As he pronounced the term *homo ludens,* Brother Isidore Leis, seated not far from Father Louis, whipped out a box of cough drops, pointed to the name Ludens and nodded knowingly, as if to show Father Louis that he was up to the minute. This example of monastic humor amused Merton all of that rainy day.

December

More of the profoundest kind of joy came to him with a meeting beginning December 3 with a group of fifteen contemplative nuns who spent four days at Gethsemani in conference. Father Louis was impressed by their quality—"completely simple, honest, authentic people." He had never felt such a sense of community with any group. "We had a really first rate session, ending with Mass together at the hermitage ... and such a Mass as you never saw; all joined in to give bits of the homily, to utter petitions at the prayer of the people."[17]

In his journal he referred to the Mass as "unutterably good, something I simply can't articulate," and mentioned that his four days with the sisters had left him with a sense of being "completely renewed."

On Thursday, Father Louis walked down to see the sisters on their way. One car after another drove away, "and finally the green station wagon from New Orleans roaring off with Sister Kathleen at the wheel. The last I saw of her she was barreling down the middle of the highway."

Father Louis's only other visitors during December were professional colleagues who had become friends. The second Sunday in Advent, December 10, the Meatyards and Wendell Berry with his wife, Tania, brought Denise Levertov to the monastery. Since it was raining, Merton took them up to the hermitage for the afternoon. He had the highest esteem for the poetry of Denise Levertov, and liked her immediately as a person. The group spent the afternoon discussing poetry and poets and photographers and Father Merton's plans for *Monks Pond.*

With their departure the monk began a period of fasting and retreat. This hardly diminished his workload, but it was work for which he had great enthusiasm. He combined his Christmas cards to his professional colleagues with announcements about *Monks Pond.* These cards were printed up in a stark black and white design with the words "Into this world, this demented inn, Christ comes uninvited." After wishing one of his correspondents a good Christmas, he added, "Look, I am starting a magazine — 4 issues only — can you let me have a few hot pages? Poetry & Prose — offbeat. I want to collect some marvelous things & already have some. Anyone you can think of? How about Brad Daniel? Where's John Beecher now?"

The forthcoming election of a new abbot for Gethsemani preoccupied him as it did all of the monks. He had no intention of ever allowing himself to be drafted as an abbot, and in his regular Sunday conference on December 17 he announced that if by chance, anyone had an idea of casting a vote for him, he wanted it known that he would under no circumstances accept the job. He also posted on the bulletin board a facetious statement explaining why he would not be abbot. It was entitled "MY CAMPAIGN PLATFORM for non-Abbot and permanent keeper of present doghouse."

He wrote that although he felt sure there were enough sane men in the community not to vote for him, but in case anyone was interested, he would like to set down his position in unmistakably clear terms.

1. More than ten years ago I made a private vow never to accept an Abbatial election. This vow was approved by Dom James and the Abbot General, Dom Gabriel Sortais, both of whom accepted it with evident relief as a sign of the Lord's mercy and of His continued determination to protect the Order from disaster. I consider myself permanently bound by this vow and believe that under no circumstances should I consent to a dispensation.

2. My reasons: a) My vocation is to the solitary life plus a certain amount of writing. Indications have long since made it morally certain that this is what our Lord asks of me. To accept the Abbatial office and dignity would be an infidelity to my true calling.

b) I would be completely incapable of assuming the duties of a superior, since I am in no sense an administrator still less a business man. Nor am I equipped to spend the rest of my life arguing about complete trivialities with one hundred twenty five slightly confused and anxiety ridden monks. The responsibility of presiding over anything larger than a small chicken coop is beyond my mental, moral and physical capacities.

c) Even if I did once cherish a few ideas about possibilities of monastic development, these have by now become foggy and indistinct, due to the encroachments of age and mental deterioration. In any case I always knew that *nothing* I might be interested in could be accomplished in a large, well established and highly official institution.

d) Since I have been a constant and unfailing disedification to the community for twenty-six years, it is obvious that anyone voting for me would have to be in a dubious condition spiritually. You would probably be voting for me on the grounds that I would grant you plenty of beer. Well, I would, but it takes more than that to make a good Abbot.

e) I cannot think of any single thing connected with the office of Abbot that makes any real sense to me in the context of my own life.

3. Consequently—in all seriousness—I feel obligated in conscience to do everything in my power to prevent this happening and to refuse it if it happens. I cannot under any circumstances agree that I should accept an election as Abbot. My vow and my solitary life are the divine will for me.

4. I apologize once again for putting something like this on paper, but it would be even more embarrassing to have to talk about it *viva voce*. And of course I do realize that the matter is not that urgent: few would be tempted to waste their votes on me in any case. If you threw the paper away without reading it, you missed nothing. If you got this far without feeling physically indisposed, pray for me. Otherwise, see Fr. Eudes—and pray for me anyhow. *Tu autem Domine miserere nobis* (note conservative trend)

Your brother in Christ,
br m louis

Some of the community did not find this amusing and did not fail to reproach him for the notice. After his astonishment that anyone could take his paper seriously, Father Louis regretted any offense he might have given. "Apparently what troubled most was the sentence where I said I did not want to spend the rest of my life arguing about complete trivialities 'with 125 confused and anxiety-ridden monks' ... At least I should keep my mouth shut, be more considerate and also stay out of their way."

On December 23, Father Louis gave the hermitage a thorough cleaning in preparation for Christmas. This would be their first Christmas in the new abbey church. In his Advent-Christmas letter to his friends, he spoke of the renovation as a great artistic success "with all the simplicity and clean-cut grace a true Cistercian Church should have. Much credit is due to the architect William Schickel."

In this same letter, he spoke of his sorrow over the death of his friends— Victor Hammer, Ad Reinhardt and John Slate. And he repeated what he had so often said before.

One of the main purposes of this printed letter is to try to say "No" tactfully to so many people who imagine I am able to undertake a steady correspondence, or receive them as visitors, or take them on in spiritual direction by mail. I am sorry, but it is just impossible for me to do any of these things. I have an immense amount of mail, and some of it I can't even read myself, let alone answer. I try to do the best I can, and obviously I have to write letters about my work. These alone are enough to keep me very busy ... I am repeatedly having to refuse invitations to go out and give talks or attend seminars and conferences. It is not possible for me to do these things ... For me it would be a waste of time. I have better ways of communicating with the outside world, I believe, and I can't envisage a life spent dashing here and there on planes. It is not what I came here for.

The night of December 23 turned bitterly cold. Father Louis stepped out on the porch and stood there, absorbed in the bright stars, the frozen woods, the silence.

Christmas Eve Mass in the new church impressed the monk as particularly good with everyone alive to the spirit. Dom James preached his last sermon as abbot, "simple and quite moving."

Father Louis walked back to the hermitage in the darkness, tired from the late hour, and went to bed immediately.

After the noon meal on Christmas day, the other two hermits at Gethsemani, Father Flavian Burns and Father Hilarion Schmock came to Father Louis's hermitage for a "General Chapter of Hermits." Their conversation concerned the election of the new abbot. They felt that Father Flavian was their best possible choice and urged him not to take himself out of the running and to accept the position if he were elected.

Later in the afternoon, Father Louis walked down the hill to the residence of Mr. and Mrs. Leo Gannon, who ran the monastery guesthouses, to pay his Christmas visit. When he returned to the hermitage, the Gannons' pet dog followed him. He tried to chase the dog back home but the animal would not leave him. He let the dog outside when he went to bed and refused to feed him, thinking he would surely go back to his owners.

When the monk awakened at 3 A.M., the cabin was bitterly cold. The dog was still there, whimpering outside his door. He let the animal in. "By that time it was starved, ran in triumphantly and jumped on my bed with enormous tail-wagging and saying 'I love you—feed me.'"

As soon as it was daylight, he took the dog back to its worried owners, who were already out searching for it.

1968

---❖---

In My End Is My Beginning

In the Beginning of Beginnings was Void of Void,
the Nameless. And in the Nameless was the One,
without body, without form.
This one — this Being in whom all find power to exist —
Is the Living.
From the Living, comes the Formless, the Undivided.
From the act of this Formless, come the Existents,
each according to its inner principal.
This is Form. Here body embraces and cherishes spirit.
The two work together as one, blending
and manifesting their characters. And this is Nature.

But he who obeys Nature returns through Form
and Formless to the Living,
and in the Living
joins the unbegun Beginning.
The joining is Sameness. The Sameness is Void.
The Void is infinite.
The bird opens its beak and sings its note
and then the beak comes together again in Silence.
So Nature and the Living meet together in Void.
Like the closing of the bird's beak after its song.

Heaven and earth come together in the Unbegun,
and all is foolishness, all is unknown, all is like
the lights of an idiot, all is without mind!
To obey is to close the beak and fall into Unbeginning.

— Translated by Thomas Merton
The Way of Chuang Tzu

January

January 1968 began bright and cold. Father Louis walked among trees "hard and sparkling with snow." The day's brilliance appeared almost perverse to him in contrast to his somber premonitions of the year to come, "a year of darkness, wetness, ice and cold and the scent of illness."

In his hermitage he opened Fitzgerald's translation of Homer to page 81 and copied this passage in his notebook:

> ... you shall not die in the bluegrass land of Argos:
> rather the gods intend you for Elysion
> with golden Rhadamanthus at the world's end ...

At dusk the monk went out again and said Compline to the accompanying crackle of frozen snow under his rubber boots. He stopped near the edge of the forest and gazed out over the valley for a long while as twilight faded to night under a new moon. Chilled, he turned back to his cabin. After stirring up the fire, he wrote in his journal, "Who is entitled to such peace? I don't know, but I would be foolish to leave it for no good reason."

As the date for the election of the new abbot approached, Father Louis expressed concern that they might select someone unsympathetic to his aspirations.

> However, the real issue is not how easy or hard it may be to get on with the next abbot, but the honesty and faith of my own commitment. The need to concentrate on the *main thing*. Still needs clarifying.
>
> It is not simply a matter of saying I have vows here. Certainly, I mean to keep my vows and stay within the order, also to live up, as far as possible, to my hermit commitment.

Early on the morning of January 13 he walked down the hill to the abbey to vote in the election. Between ballots the cloister was filled with silent monks reading. "I read long chunks of David Jones' *Anathemata*, somehow very moving and sonorous in that charged silence, and one felt a blessing over it all even before any idea how it would turn out. It was all over by 9:30. By that time it was snowing again."

Father Flavian Burns was elected abbot by a large majority on the third ballot.

The following day Father Louis made his promise of obedience "with a great sense of meaning—a sense of authentic *human* possibilities in context of real friendship among all those of Flavian's generation and who will collaborate with him now."

A severe case of the flu struck down Father Louis the next day. He decided to medicate himself in the hermitage rather than go to the infirmary at the abbey. He remained in bed covered with blankets for three days, "aching and smashed in stupid sleep."

By the nineteenth he was getting up, but still sick, "with a dry cough, gut in shambles, high fever, nauseated by everything, unable to say office or do anything whatever except occasionally get up to make tea and take a pill." The next morning he felt strong enough to say Lauds and Mass before the cold sweats and weakness drove him back to bed. At noon he prepared some soup and eggs, looked out at the dazzling light of sun on snow and began to revive.

He wrote in his journal:

An experience like the sickness is purifying and renewing, because it reminds you not to get too attached to the narrow view of what you think life is—the immediate task, the business of getting done what you think is important ... Sickness pulls the rug out from under all of it. I haven't been able to do anything, think anything. Yet in the evening—the bare trees against the metallic blue of the evening were incredibly beautiful: as suspended in a kind of Buddhist emptiness.

The next afternoon he celebrated his recovery by going "for the first decent walk in almost a week—out to the pond by St. Bernard's field with its green ice and dead trees and silences." In the evening, he stacked a three-record set of Mozart Quintets, played by the Budapest Quartet with violist Walter Trampler, on a portable record player borrowed from the monastery. He was listening to the music while cooking his supper when he heard a loud knock. Opening the door he saw Brother Thomas Arthron, who had come to tell him that his friend Seymour (Sy) Freedgood was dead.

Father Louis quickly slipped into his denim jacket and boots and hurried down to the abbey to telephone Mrs. Freedgood. Although he could not speak with her, one of her friends at her New York apartment explained that the Freedgoods' house in Bridgehampton had burned during the night and that Sy had been unable to get out. Father Louis sent a telegram to Robert Lax and then trudged back up the hill to his cabin.

He opened the door to the sounds of Mozart and the fragrance of a wood fire burning low in his fireplace. The monk turned off the record player and replaced the records in the album. "I no longer feel like listening to anything," he wrote. "Mozart or anything else." He saw Freedgood's death as the first confirmation of his New Year's premonition that 1968 would be a year of tragedy.

"It is already a hard year, and I don't know what else is coming, but I have a feeling it is going to be a hard year all the way and for everybody."

Father Louis mourned his friend. In the days that followed, his notebooks filled with recollections and with the term "Poor Sy!"

Mass for him yesterday in the library chapel, and today in the hermitage. I remember so many things. Sy and Rice at my baptism ... Sy trying to teach me judo on a sandbar in the lagoon behind Long Beach ...

Last year he was here looking terrible in his fur hat and bandaged face and I knew he was finished. Yet he was full of ideas and plans.

A week of intrusions and interruptions preceded the monk's fifty-third birthday on January 31. He had to go into Louisville for an examination by his proctologist. While in town he visited Tommie O'Callaghan, who was recovering at home from recent surgery. There he saw, and was deeply impressed by, photographs of the O'Callaghan children made by Ralph Eugene Meatyard. He also procured the Impulse recording of John Coltrane's *Ascension*, "which is shattering. A fantastic and prophetic piece of music." He decided to use it for priests conferences.

He spent almost the entire morning of Friday, January 26, attempting to bring some order to his mail,

though this is harder and harder to do. So much of the mail seems completely pointless ... And in fact a great deal of it is chiefly a matter of someone trying to get your name for something, to line you up for some cause or other, or to engage you in a chain of pseudo events and pseudo decisions: or more simply: to get some money out of you: or to use you in some way.

He took a long walk that afternoon.

I had a book in my pocket and couldn't read a line of it. Only looked at the sun ... the blue sky, and felt utterly blank. Will there never be any peace on earth in our lifetime? Will they never do anything but kill, and then kill some more? Apparently they are caught in that impasse: the system is completely violent and involved in violence: and that leads only to more violence. Really—what is ahead but the Apocalypse?

Throughout the day of Wednesday, January 31, his birthday, the silence of the hermitage and surrounding forests turned ominous because of the distant booming of artillery from Ft. Knox.

Clear thin new moon appearing and disappearing between sage blue clouds and the living black skeletons of the trees against the evening sky. It is my fifty-third birthday.

We do not have a war—only the "Pueblo crisis" with senators shouting like complete morons about "wiping the yellow bastards off the map" or words to that effect. Complete insanity.

But the guns at Knox nevertheless shake all my windows.

February

Father Louis was often fascinated by the people who came to the abbey and asked to see him. But they placed a severe strain on his solitary vocation and work schedule. On Friday afternoon, February 2, when he was absorbed in work, a friend showed up unexpectedly with Father Malcolm Boyd. Merton noted that he was glad to meet Father Boyd, "yet felt I talked too much and too wildly—or anyway too irresponsibly, perhaps overcompensating for the fact that I had rather *not* have been visited."

Certain visits were necessary, and these were always cleared well in advance. "But," Merton wrote in his journal,

> a lot of them are simply bursting in uninvited and are a nuisance. And going to town is a bigger nuisance. True, I have to see the doctor, and there are other things to do, but more and more I have a sense of untruth and ambiguity in all my "social" existence, from my conferences in the monastery to visits with people from outside. A few rare exceptions.

In addition to visits and mail, Father Louis began to get more inquiries from people who wondered if, with the new abbot, he would be given freedom to travel, attend meetings and give lectures or retreats. Not only was Dom Flavian just as opposed to that as Dom James had been, but Merton himself felt it would be futile and irrelevant for him, and a falsification of his vocation.

"I need quiet. I need to get down to more reading and meditation. The problem of people is of my own making—as problem and as ambiguity."

On the Feast of St. Romauld, February 8, he received a mimeo copy of his early novel, as yet unpublished, *Journal of My Escape from the Nazis.*[1]

"Whatever the mess, this is a book I am pleased with," he wrote in his notebook. "Not that it holds together perfectly as a book, but there is good writing and it comes from the center where I have really experienced myself and my life . . . Perhaps I am now returning to some such moment of great truth. I hope I am. I won't have many more chances!"

James Laughlin arrived the same day to help Merton with details for establishing the Merton Legacy Trust. The two men spent the afternoon and all of the following day working on the Trust indenture. They met on Friday with attorney John Ford and Mrs. Frank O'Callaghan to complete all of the paperwork dealing with copyrights, rules for commissions and other business details. Father Merton concluded that "libraries and publishers like rules as much as monks do, in effect more."

By Saturday, February 10, Father Louis was once again alone in the hermitage. The weather turned bitterly cold. In late afternoon, after finishing a batch of letters to poets who had submitted contributions to *Monks Pond* — a correspondence the monk enjoyed — he walked outside to say his office. "The moon was up and two deer were standing motionless out in the middle of the field, watching me, their ears spread out, their grey winter coats almost green against the field."

The temperature stayed between zero and twenty degrees, bringing a halt to visits. Father Louis settled back into his work, noting that it was "very cold, very silent when I was out during meditation — only a distant train. To have only one far noise is now equivalent to silence."

New invitations arrived. Dom Jean Leclercq informed Father Louis and Abbot Flavian of a meeting of Asian abbots scheduled for Bangkok, Thailand, in December. This meeting for monastic superiors in the Far East, was to be held under the sponsorship of an international Benedictine organization, *Aide a l'Implantation Monastique* (A. I. M.) headquartered in Paris. Dom Leclercq urged Father Merton to make an exception and consider seriously the importance of participating in this meeting. The monk thought about it at length and discussed it with Abbot Flavian, without coming to any definite decision.

In late February, Dom Flavian handed Merton a blue envelope from the British Broadcasting Corporation containing an invitation for the monk to be interviewed by Malcolm Muggeridge for TV. "Obviously turned down," Father Louis wrote. "I am suggesting to Father Flavian that Muggeridge should nevertheless stop by here for an informal visit."

Father Louis was named to the Monastic Council and attended council meeting at the abbey on February 24.

> Quiet, reasonable, a very good atmosphere of peace, charity, sense. Father Flavian is impressive as abbot. ... Under Dom James my struggles and exasperations led me to do wrong and unwise things without clearly seeing what I was doing — and thinking myself justified. Under Dom Flavian I am interested in being more honest and more serious — and a better hermit. It will be a struggle because I have let things get potentially out of hand by thoughtlessness and carelessness with people, visitors, etc. Just to aim at moderation does not really work ... In the end, something more absolute is required — and more real solitude.

With the unrelenting cold, the monk began to long for spring, and to perceive hints of its promise. "In the evening the bare trees have a certain way of bearing themselves up against the blue late sky, as if they knew for sure the promise of sap in them. I sang the *Te Lucis* and realized it is a lovely hymn."

The following morning, long before dawn, he stood outside and read the office by the porch light. "Snowflakes melt on the pages of the breviary.

Empty belly. Down in the monastery they now have English vigils. I cling to the Latin. I need the continuity," he wrote.

Later in the day he finished writing "The Study of Zen," which he felt concluded his work on the book *Zen and the Birds of Appetite,* and began getting the entire manuscript ready to mail to James Laughlin.

March

On March 1 the first issue of *Monks Pond* was printed. Father Louis walked down to the monastery to help arrange and staple the pages for mailing.

The community decided that the hermit should have an addition to the cabin — a 6' x 8' room to serve as a chapel and an even smaller bathroom, just large enough to crowd in a wash basin, toilet and shower, both rooms opening into the kitchen.

As the weather cleared and the first crocuses bloomed at the foot of the tall cross in front of his cabin, Father Louis began to spend more time meditating in the woods. He found an isolated spot he had never visited before, "a rocky scrubby hollow across Monk's Creek next to the old Linton place near Flavian's hermitage." He sat in the sun, read Eckhart and said Vespers. "What else really is there? I really enjoyed being in that wild silent spot where no one as yet goes. It is very much out of the way — and I am aware I will need an out-of-the-way-place like that to hide in if too many people start coming to the hermitage on summer afternoons.

"And really I am ready to let the writing go to the dogs, if necessary, and to prefer this: that is what I really want and what I am here for."

With the beginning of Lent, Father Louis enjoyed several weeks of near-perfect silence and solitude. The weather remained cold. Each morning he awakened to find a hard frost and the water in the buckets frozen solid. But the cold was different, he noted. The sun came up bright and he heard spring bird songs even in the snow. The frogs were silent until the noon sun melted the ice. "They then sing in the afternoon."

In anticipation of the spring and summer, the monk began to revise his schedule. He no longer took it for granted that the afternoon was for writing, "just because that is the way it had to be in the community."

He decided to do most of his writing early in the morning. Then in the afternoon he could go into the woods and thus be away from the hermitage at the time when people might be tempted to visit him.

Merton's writings on peace, social justice and racism continued to scandalize and outrage those Christians who viewed any criticism of America as unpatriotic and therefore unchristian.

"Ever increasing frenzy, tension, explosiveness in this century," the monk wrote in his journal.

People in Detroit buying guns. Vigilante groups being formed to shoot Negroes . . . This is really a mad country, and an explosion of madness is inevitable. The only question — can it somehow be *less bad* than one anticipates? Total chaos is quite possible, though I don't anticipate that. But the fears, frustrations, hatreds, irrationalities, mysteries, are all there, and all powerful enough to blow everything wide open.

Attacks against Merton continued in letters directly to him, or in letters to Catholic magazines and newspapers. "More attacks in *The Record* [Louisville Archdiocesan newspaper]," Father Louis noted on March 15. "A devout Catholic is burning my books. I must be Godless, I wish to save lives rather than 'kill commies for Christ.' Went out again to my small west pond and did some Zen. It was right. When I came back, I saw two cars waiting by my gate. I hid in the cedars until three priests appeared. Disappointed, they drove off and I returned to the hermitage."

The chapel-bathroom addition to the cabin went up slowly. By March 20, Merton noted that the walls were raised. On that same day, he received typewritten transcripts of some of the tapes he had made for various groups of sisters. Reading them was a sobering experience.

The result is an appalling semi-articulate mishmash of sentences that doesn't end, or vanishes in mid-air, of clichés, idiot colloquialisms, vague suppositions, intuitions that don't get anywhere, feeble humor, etc. It is good to see how bad this kind of thing can get. How sloppy, how untrue to my real thinking in many ways.

A violent snow storm the day and night of March 22 threatened the hermitage and kept the monk up much of the night. While he was taking his supper, two tall pines in front of the cabin crashed down from the weight of the snow. He heard others fall deep in the forest. Afraid to go to bed, he sat up late, hoping the storm would subside.

The next morning he noted,

A strange and difficult night. Snow continued to fall most of the night and I could hear the big trees hanging over the house cracking with their load. I slept with all my clothes on, coat and shoes, in case my bedroom should suddenly be filled with snowy branches and pieces of the roof.

When the monk went down to the abbey to pick up his mail the next morning, he found a package containing a 35 mm Canon FX Camera with a 50mm and a 100mm lens. For some time he had been interested in photography and had used borrowed cameras of varying quality, sending the negatives to Gregory Griffin for processing and printing. His gifts as a photographer were of a high order. It was decided that he would accept the loan of proper equipment for his own use.

"Your letter about the camera was one of the most exciting things that ever happened," he wrote John Howard Griffin. He continued,

> THE most exciting was the arrival of the camera itself. It is superb. I haven't had a chance to take it out, though we have some nice afternoons: I have had a lot of people here and problems to sweat out. So far I have only read the instructions, procured film and become acquainted with the different gadgets. What a thing to have around! I will take reverent care of it, and any time you want it . . . I will take good care to see that it goes straight back to you if anything happens to me.[2]

Two days later he wrote again.

> What a joy of a thing to work with. I am sending the first two rolls and hoping that they are ok, that I haven't done something all wrong: but the camera is the most eager and helpful of beings, all full of happy suggestions: "Try this! Do it that way." Reminding me of things I have overlooked, and cooperating in the creation of new worlds. So simply. This is a Zen camera. As for the F.100, I tell you I'm going to blow my mind with it![3]

By the end of March, Merton acknowledged his irritation with some of the books he felt obliged to read, books he might have found fascinating a few years earlier. Writing of Rahner's *Theology of Proclamation,* he observed, "Probably there is a point in it somewhere later, something important. But he is trying to convince theologians and bishops, and I am neither. Why bother reading him? (Though I have in the past liked some of his stuff, viz *The Dynamic Element in the Church.*)"

He could not recall the titles of the dozen other books he had given up on recently. All of them, he said, were important books, but they bored him now. At the same time, he received five books on and one by James Joyce, which he agreed to review for the *Sewanee Review.* He remarked, "It was exciting to get back in touch with Joyce after all these years."

Also in late March, Father Louis received a copy of *The Essential Lenny Bruce*[4] as a gift from Lionel Landry of the Asia Society in New York. He wrote Landry immediately.

> I looked straight at the back and found that actually what he did was a marvelous adaptation of a much longer and more intricate poem of mine. His was the same poem, but cut down to a series of left hooks for the night club or wherever he did it, and much funnier. My own is very dour and quiet, this is rambunctious and wild.

People like Lenny Bruce are really monks in reverse and hence I feel much closer to them than I do to say the President of General Motors.[5]

Lawrence Schiller, in his book *Ladies and Gentlemen: Lenny Bruce*[6] says, "Some nights he would end his act with a bit that had no precedent in the history of American nightclub humor. It was *inspired* by a poem of Thomas Merton, which Lenny had read and treasured for a couple of years."

Bruce's routine was based on "A Devout Meditation in Memory of Adolf Eichmann," with overtones from "Chant to Be Used in Procession around a Site with Furnaces."

April

On a cloudy Thursday afternoon, April 4, Father Louis accompanied two guests to Shakertown to show them the Shaker Museum and make photographs. They drove into Lexington and stopped at Lum's for supper. On the TV news, they saw a clip of Martin Luther King, Jr., who had talked the previous night in Memphis. "I was impressed by his tenseness and strength. A sort of vague, visceral, auditory impression," the monk noted later. He was also interested in the TV account of the white man in South Africa who had undergone the first successful heart transplant. "He had an African Negro's heart in him, beating along. They asked him if he felt any different toward his wife and I nearly fell off my chair laughing. No one else could figure out what was funny."

Almost immediately after leaving the restaurant to drive back to Gethsemani, they heard on the car radio that Martin Luther King, Jr., had been shot and was in critical condition. Long before they reached Bardstown they learned King had died.

Merton felt that the murder of Martin Luther King, Jr., lay on top of the traveling car like an animal, a beast of the Apocalypse.

Rainy night. Big, columned Baptist churches. Highway with huge lights and wrong turns. Radio. Nashville. Louisville. Indianapolis. Jazz. News. Ads. M. L. King gradually coming clear through all the rock and roll as definitively *dead*.

In Bardstown Merton decided to stop by and offer his condolences to Colonel Hawkes. The Colonel, a famous black restauranteur and longtime friend of the monks of Gethsemani, received him with open arms and great sadness. They sat together in an empty side room of the restaurant and talked for almost three hours. "Hawkes, with his arm around me saying, 'This is my *boy*, this is my *friend*.' I could cry."

The murder of Martin Luther King, Jr., confirmed all of Father Louis's apprehensions that 1968 was a beast of a year. "Things are finally, inexorably spelling themselves out. Why? Are things happening because people in desperation *want* them to happen? . . . Is the Christian message of love a pitiful delusion? Or must one just 'love' in an impossible situation?"

Father Louis went into Louisville on Saturday to the O'Callaghans to hear Alex Peloquin's musical settings of Merton's "Four Freedom Songs."[7] "The songs are good, though, should make a good TV show. They were to have been presented at the Liturgical Conference at which M. L. King was to have been present."

By mid-April the problem of real solitude had become acute for Father Louis.

> I am not really living as a hermit. I see too many people, have too much active work to do, the place is too noisy, too accessible. People are always coming up here, and I have been too slack about granting visits, interviews, etc. All I have is a certain privacy, but real solitude is less and less possible here. Everyone now knows where the hermitage is. In May I am going to the Convent of the Redwoods in California. Once I start traveling around, what hope will there be?

Brother Benedict Kunz, who was then guestmaster, recalls how the monks tried to protect Father Louis from those intruders, who were determined to see him, with or without permission:

> I think that most of us were on the lookout for Louie's welfare . . . People would ask where his hermitage was, and not getting the answer, but one which told them Louie's privacy had to be respected, would then ask even for the general direction of his hermitage. Even this was not divulged. Most of us did not wander around his hermitage ourselves because we knew this would disturb him and was not the right thing to do. We wanted him to have his solitude . . . I think it was Louie's own fault that the hermitage lost its solitude for him. He would invite people up to the hermitage, and they of course would later think it okay to visit him, or tell their friends how to get to the hermitage when the friends wanted to see Louie.

The hermit described the morning of April 25 as "one of those than which no more beautiful is possible." But when he went down to get his mail, he found a rolled-up newspaper from New Zealand describing a freak accident in which a ferry sank in the entrance to Wellington Harbor. In the list of those who died, he saw the name Agnes Gertrude Merton, 79, Christchurch.

"Poor Aunt Kit!" he wrote. "It happened April 10, two weeks ago, Wednesday in Holy Week. And no one had told me about it. I said Mass for her—the Mass of the Holy Cross."

That afternoon he did a minimum of work "and went out to mourn quietly, walking in the bottoms. The need to lament, to express and offer up sorrow and loss."

Later he reread everything in the paper, the complete accounts of the accident. "A frightful mess. And in the middle of it all poor sweet Aunt Kit, old and without strength to fight a cold, wild sea. I look at the sweater she knitted me to protect me against 'the cole' and the whole thing is unbearable."

Two days later, the hermitage chapel was finished. The monk stayed up late, cleaning the room, putting up his icons in preparation for his first Mass there on Saturday morning. He felt that having a separate little room for his chapel made a great difference. He began celebrating his Masses and saying most of the hours of the office in that room.

May

His first prolonged absence from Gethsemani took him to the Trappistine convent Our Lady of the Redwoods, in Whitehorn, California, where he gave seminars and conferences to the sisters. There, he found almost more solitude than he now had at the hermitage. He spent four days of complete solitude in a small farm house near Bear Harbor, "the isolated cove on the Pacific shore where the Jones house is . . . the barns, the sheep, the Eucalyptus trees, the steep slopes crowned by fir, the cove full of drift redwood logs, black sand, black stones, and restless sea . . . I seem to remember every inch of that shore." These were days of unutterable happiness, he said, and he hoped some means might be found to rent the Jones' house so that he could return there perhaps for Lent each year.

On May 16, Mother Miriam, superior of Our Lady of the Redwoods, drove him to San Francisco where he called Lawrence Ferlinghetti. The poet joined them for lunch in an Italian restaurant, then took Merton to an expresso house in North Beach and later to the City Lights Publication office, where the monk spent the night.

Returning to Gethsemani he made one more stop to visit the Monastery of Christ in the Desert at Abiquiu, New Mexico, recalling its "arrogant, flop-eared Nubian goats, cared for by a Cistercian hermit from Snowmass," and the beauty of the wild countryside.

After a series of flight delays, Father Louis arrived back in Louisville late in the evening, May 20. He spent the remainder of the night in the O'Callaghan home and was driven back to the abbey the next morning by his friend Ron Seitz.

The news came through on May 28 that Father Philip Berrigan, S.S.J., had been sentenced to six years in prison for pouring blood on the draft files in Baltimore, and that he would also be tried, along with his brother, Father Daniel Berrigan, S.J., for burning other draft files.

"Six years! It is a bit of a shock to find one's friends so concretely and tangibly on the outs with society." He concluded that both Phil and Dan were being persecuted for saying openly what more and more Americans were beginning to believe — that the U.S. was becoming a totalitarian society.

Their way of saying it is a bit blunt, and a lot of people are so dazed by the statement that they don't grasp it at all. Those of us who do grasp it are, to say the least, sobered. If, in fact, I basically agree with them, then how long will I myself be out of jail? I suppose I can say "as long as I don't make a special effort to get in" — which is what they did. All I can say is that I haven't deliberately broken any laws. But one of these days I may find myself in a position where I will have to.

EPILOGUE

At the beginning of his book *Raids on the Unspeakable,* Thomas Merton cited a key passage from Gabriel Marcel.

Today the first and perhaps the only duty of the philosopher is to defend man against himself: to defend man against that extraordinary temptation toward inhumanity to which—almost without being aware of it—so many humans today have yielded.

On his own, the middle-aged monk had gradually arrived at the same conclusion and had written extensively and courageously about most of the "controversial" themes that illuminated that "extraordinary temptation toward inhumanity" and the general dehumanization that resulted from yielding to that temptation. It took courage in those days to speak independently about issues such as racism, monastic reform, human rights, nuclear proliferation, and human freedom from programming—all those issues on which criticism or even analysis could and still can so exacerbate partisan emotions. Most of these were issues about which a contemplative monk might ordinarily remain safely silent, but Thomas Merton followed his conscience and his insights, and it cost him much in the way of esteem. True, many saw hope in his voice and viewed him as prophetic. But many others who might admire his "spiritual" writings came to consider him a radical, a subversive and that greatest of social sinners, "a trouble-maker," because of his more controversial writings during the sixties.

Merton personally disliked controversy as much as anyone I have ever known. Yet he had those remarkable insights that made him see deeper than most of us, and in conscience he had to speak out, even when it produced the hostility that hurt him deeply.

Archbishop Dom Helder Camara of Brazil refers to such people as the "Abrahamic Minority." The world has always been saved by this minority. One would instantly think of Schweitzer, Einstein and Gandhi in this context. Merton would have added Pasternak, Camus and Maritain—as well as countless other lesser-known but no less authentic members. I think particularly of Father Dominique Pire, awarded the Nobel Peace Prize for his aid to Displaced Persons in World War II, and Dr. Martin Luther King. It was a great privilege working with these fighters against racism and war. It was also a great lesson. There have always been a few who, in time of great trouble, are keenly aware of the underlying tragedy: the needless destruction of humankind. This minority gives every ounce to compensate for the lack of awareness in the majority. This minority diminishes, but when it disappears, it won't be the end of humanity. It will be the end of humankind as we know it. Justice has now become a biological necessity in human beings, as J. Bronowski commented just before he died. It isn't a matter of choice, but biological necessity. The "Abrahamic Minority" keeps this justice alive. Dr. Viktor Frankl speaks of this minority as "the decent, human or humane ones who will always remain an absolute minority."

In "Rain and Rhinoceros," Merton observed, "Only the man who has fully attained his own spiritual identity can live without the need to kill, and without the need of a spiritual doctrine that permits him to do so in good conscience." He also said, toward the end of his life, "If you are going to be yourself, you are not going to fit anybody else's mystique." This is a most profound clue to his independence, and one of the reasons his friends, coreligionists and even his colleagues in the "Abrahamic Minority" sometimes judged him incorrectly. Before you could be yourself, however, Merton felt you had to take the time alone to become yourself, to face yourself in your fundamental reality, and to peel away the accretions of mediocre or false values imposed by society, ambition and self-interest. Only then, as the overflow of such contemplation could you find your truth and your reality.

I recall a young priest from Mississippi who visited the monastery of Gethsemani at the same time I did in the early sixties. This priest spoke with Merton and me about his torment over the segregation of churches in his area. "I know it's wrong," he said. "Sometimes I can hardly face myself in the mirror in the mornings for going along with it. What can I do?"

"Don't do a damned thing," Merton replied sympathetically. "Just take the time to become what you profess to be. Then you will know what to do."

This meant taking the time to become fully himself in all his truth before deciding on an action. The monk replied, too, that the young priest had to arrive at decisions of such gravity within himself. Having lived through the days of Nazi oppression, having seen racism at close hand in this country, having witnessed the establishment's suppression and character-assassination of those opposing United States involvement in the Vietnam war, and having worked with those struggling for human rights and peace, Thomas Merton realized that ethics based on consensus and expediency, rather than on principle, produced societies of a monolithic mediocrity that always sought to destroy what they could not encompass.

The decision to face reprisals for the good of those who would persecute him had to be a person's own. Merton would not make such decisions for others, nor would he judge those who simply could not make those sacrifices; he commiserated deeply with those who attempted the sacrifice and caved in when reprisals were brought against them.

His fidelity to his particular and individual vocation was perhaps the most difficult thing for many, including those many whom he supported, to understand. Many activists felt that Father Louis should be out of the cloister and into the streets "where the action was," and could be quite obnoxious in telling him so. We were in the "real world," they seemed to think, which at least implied that the monk was not. Others of us in the streets, however, understood and treasured Merton's vocation—it helped us to persevere when so many were dropping away. I have often said that we could not have done what we did without dedicated souls in monasteries and convents to back us up. Merton was anchored in reality and we looked to him to help us keep our balance and our sense of reality. Many of us could vouch that when desperate times came, when we seemed to be accomplishing nothing, when we were calumnied and threatened and tempted to give up, Father Louis and others like him salvaged us. We were not salvaged by the strategists or the sociologists but by men and women of highly advanced spiritual dimensions.

Merton's fidelity to this contemplative vocation was therefore critically important to those of us in the active life for remaining faithful in our vocations. Many of us, I know, felt that we were involved in little more than emergency work to hold off holocaust, but that the real, long-term civilizing and rehumanizing work was to be done by the artists, the thinkers, the prophets and the saints.

Dan Berrigan refers to people such as Merton as our "readers of clues." One realizes now, over the perspective of years, that he could not have read the clues right if he had compromised his vision. Father Berrigan refers to them as the "resolute saints" in our midst, those with a simple resolve "to read things right, to tell the truth." It is not to professed religious persons Berrigan specifically alludes, but to those in whatever station of life who make up the "Abrahamic Minority."

All of this implied a side of Merton little known or understood by his critics—his belief in the quest for true interior freedom. Freedom meant a willingness to realize and experience his life as "totally absurd" (his own expression) in relation to the apparent meaning thrown over life by society and by illusion. But that could only be a starting point, he noted, leading to a deeper realization of that reality in himself and in all life. This implied the capacity to see that realizing and knowing are not the same. For Thomas Merton, solitude itself was the fullness of realization.

What Merton realized, however, was that it would be meaningless if he had not also been concerned with the dehumanization of the oppressor groups, the terrible danger to the whole people of rationalizing injustice, the tragedy of inculcating prejudice and therefore violence in our children. His capacity to grasp all the nuances of such wounds—both to oppressors and the oppressed was very nearly infallible. He felt them with a depth I have rarely encountered.

When I became too ill to continue work in the active life, Thomas Merton wrote that he felt our problems of social justice and peace were beyond the capacity of human beings to solve and that only God could resolve them, that it was all in God's hands. "In this light, you may now accomplish more in the proper use of your suffering than you ever accomplished in your more active life," he declared—and he proved to be right. Of course he wasn't saying we should do nothing and give up. No, he meant that the healing of humanity's wounds is a need so vast and complex that all of us have a responsibility to any progress that may be made or hoped for, and that we must continue to remain faithful to our individual vocations in the general fabric.

It seems that the great humanizers of our lifetime have all arrived at these fundamental truths clarified for us in Thomas Merton's life and writings: the tremendous necessity of first *being* and then *doing*; and the impossibility of this without the interior freedom to transcend ourselves. Yet every single such person has been considered highly controversial and has in some way been martyred for the love of fellow human beings. The bewilderment comes from wondering what is controversial in any of this.

In those years between Thomas Merton's ordination to the priesthood as Father Louis (in 1949) and his growing celebrity as a writer, as a monk, as a spiritual thinker during the fifties and early sixties, he held tenaciously to the idea that he was not a good community man, that he had to learn from a kind of solitude, which meant physical isolation. Actually, there is a great kind of solitude in that form of monastic community, especially during the time of the Rule of Silence, which was in effect when Merton entered Gethsemani. But Merton needed a deeper solitude. In the early sixties, he was always on the lookout for that place where he might lead a life of utter simplicity. He did so even while the idea of a Trappist living as a hermit approximated a scandal.

A curious thing happened in 1964. The abbot of Mt. Savior Monastery in New York was scheduled to see the Holy Father in Rome. The abbot sent a message to Gethsemani requesting that Father Louis write a set of guidelines about monastic renewal, which the abbot would personally place in the hands of the Pontiff. Of course Merton was wide awake to this opportunity, because he was really pleading his own thoughts. He had discovered some obscure hermits in the early history of the Trappist Order, and was already at work on this idea of a hermit location within the community. In this set of guidelines, Merton said that the abbots should now be open and not perpetuate an absolute hidebound monolithic structure of community life.

During this same period, Merton was doing an enormous amount of ecumenical work. Since it was felt that religious leaders who were not Catholic might feel cut off in the guest portion of the abbey, a simple structure was built on the hill for just such conferences.

Soon Merton was allowed to enjoy the place for reading, once his duties for the day were completed. Slowly this worked into a refuge of solitude for prayer and silence. Then he was allowed to sleep there, although he continued saying his masses and teaching the novices. So, in a natural way, Merton was becoming the first modern hermit in the Trappist Order. This change significantly revitalized his life. As he was becoming increasingly famous, he was at the same time seriously retrenching from public exposure.

Thomas Merton's private journals are particularly fascinating to read at this point, because everyone was pushing him to speak, to use his influence, while he was moving toward a deeper solitude. He felt an internal spiritual connection with the great Zen poet Chuang Tzu, who wrote poems that hit Merton very deeply. The Chinese Master writes that a sense of achievement is the beginning of failure and that fame was the beginning of disgrace. Merton already believed this. Chuang Tzu, in Merton's translation, says that the authentic search for truth is to become a nobody. Only a nobody can be universal. Merton said he had disappeared into the monastery, not to get away from the world but to become a nobody.

Thus Merton entered into his first half-year as a hermit— perhaps the most gloriously happy time of his life. He was alone—without intrusions. His life was one of absolute simplicity, and it provided him with all he needed. "Without contaminating my presence with future anticipation or with facile religious consolation, I still do not live in despair because there is in me a hope which is somehow akin to a profound sense of adoration." He had come to his simple hermitage not to despair but to adore God.

Unfortunately, the hermit's solitude began to crumble in his last year. People found out where his hermitage was, and more and more invaded his solitude. He changed his entire schedule. He didn't want to be a tourist attraction. Of course, there were people who had authentic reasons to see him. So, unless there was a scheduled visitor, Merton worked in the morning, but spent the afternoons in the woods. He would return late in the evening by a way hidden from view of the hermitage. He would examine the territory for cars. Often the monk would spot intruders and wait until they were disappointed enough to drive away. This predicament led to a growing need to find some place where the hermit could live in uninterrupted silence and solitude.

It was at this time that Merton heard from an old friend, Dom Jean Leclercq, a Benedictine scholar from Luxembourg, with an invitation to participate in a meeting of Asian Abbots in Bangkok, Thailand. This served as the legal reason to make the trip. But the real purpose was for Merton to visit spiritual leaders in India and the East with a view of finding a place that the Abbey of Gethsemani might procure as a place of hermitage where monks might go for a certain portion of the year.

Merton left in September and made a prolonged trip. He was photographing immensely during that period and sending his film to my son

Gregory and me for processing. On December 8, 1968, he arrived in Bang-kok. He took a room at the Oriental Hotel. Merton wrote me a letter from the hotel, which I did not receive until after his death.

In his letter he asked a favor. He had earlier been visiting with the Dalai Lama and had sent rolls of film, which we had processed. The contact sheet we had sent excited him. In this last letter he wanted to know if I would make "a big beautiful print and send it to the Dalai Lama" with his com-pliments. He went on to say that it had been a very exciting and revealing trip. But "I have not found what I came to find. I have not found any place of hermitage that is any better than the hermitage I have, or had, at Geth-semani, which is after all places, a great place."

Of course, he did not survive his journey to the East, but died of acci-dental electrocution in Bangkok on December 10, 1968, twenty-seven years to the day after he had entered Gethsemani Abbey (December 10, 1941).

He had traveled East as a pilgrim, just as he had entered the silences of the monastery as a pilgrim. In one of his last talks, this one in Calcutta, he clarified his concerns:

> I speak as a Western monk who is pre-eminently concerned with his own monastic calling and dedication. I have left my monastery to come here not as a research scholar or even as an author (which I happen to be). I come as a pilgrim who is anxious not just to obtain infor-mation, not just *facts* about other monastic traditions, but to drink from ancient sources of monastic vision and experience. I seek not only to learn more about religion and about monastic life, but to become a better and more enlightened monk myself.

He also learned a practical but profound thing, which he mentions in *The Asian Journal:*

> The rimpoches all advise against absolute solitude and stress "com-passion." They seem to agree that being in solitude much of the year and coming "out" for a while would be a good solution.

Merton felt that this was perhaps the key to what his future would be. He greeted this fact almost as a revelation. It was such an obviously simple answer, yet one he hadn't stumbled on himself. For once it did not have to be one or the other — the monastery or the hermitage — but could be — could have been — both. And certainly his preference would have been for a longer period of solitude and shorter intervals of dialogue.

Had Thomas Merton returned from the East alive, he would have become more and more silent. He would have gone on writing forever — for he was a true poet as well as a faithful monk and priest — but he would have published less and less. He would have continued taking the authentic risks necessary to live his vocation without compromise. He had lived in an absolute way. This is courageous because he had every chance for taking the easy way out. He never did. He never wavered from his true vocation: to be always leaping over the cliffs of the spiritual life.

❖

In his Calcutta address Thomas Merton made the point that

the deepest level of communication is not communication, but communion. It is wordless. It is beyond words. It is beyond speech and it is beyond concept. Not that we discover a new unity. We discover an older unity. My dear brothers, we are already one. But we imagine that we are not. And what we have to recover is our original unity. What we have to be is what we are.

❖

The ancients said, therefore:

> *"The man of Tao*
> *Remains unknown*
> *Perfect virtue*
> *Produces nothing*
> *'No-Self'*
> *Is 'True-Self.'*
> *And the greatest man*
> *Is Nobody."*
>
> — *Chuang Tzu*
> Translated by Thomas Merton

NOTES

1965

1. Schema 13 became the historic council document, *Gaudium et Spes*, the Pastoral Constitution on the Church in the Modern World.

2. Jacques Cabaud, *Simone Weil: A Fellowship in Love* (London: Harvill Press, 1964).

3. Transcript of talk given August 20, 1965. Unpublished.

4. Father Chrysogonus Waddell, letter to author, December 3, 1971.

5. Thomas Merton, letter to James Laughlin, November 2, 1965.

6. Thomas Merton, letter to John Heidbrink, November 20, 1965.

1966

1. Thomas Merton, *Cables to the Ace* (New York: New Directions, 1968).

2. Thomas Merton, letter to James Laughlin, June 9, 1966. From the James Laughlin files.

3. Nhat Hanh, "For My Brother." In *Vietnam Poems*, trans. Helen Coutant and Nhat Hanh (Greensboro, NC: Unicorn Press, 1967).

4. *Perfectae Caritatis*, no. 14. In *The Documents of Vatican II*, ed. Walter M. Abbott, S. J. (New York: Guild Press, 1966).

5. Monastic archives, Abbey of Gethsemani.

6. David Steindl-Rast, *Monastic Studies* (1969).

7. Religious Dimensions in Literature series (New York: Seabury Press, 1968).

8. Karl Rahner, *The Dynamic Element in the Church* (New York: Herder and Herder, 1964).

9. These were later published under the title *Cables to the Ace.*

1967

1. Dr. Francis J. Paisel, note to Father John Eudes, January 3, 1967. From the files of Father John Eudes Bamberger, Abbey of Gethsemani archives.

2. Romano Guardini, *Pascal for Our Time*, trans. Brian Thompson (New York: Herder and Herder, 1966).

3. Thomas Merton, Septuagesima letter to his friends, 1967.

4. Father M. Bernard, letter to Thomas Merton, January 24, 1967. Monastic archives, Abbey of Gethsemani.

5. Father Abbot James Fox, letter to Father Louis, January 31, 1967. Monastic archives, Abbey of Gethsemani.

6. Sidi Abdesalam, letter to Thomas Merton, February 14, 1967. Bellarmine archives.

7. These drawings are in the Nancy O'Callaghan collection.

8. Louis Zukofsky, *"A" 1-12* (London: Jonathan Cape, 1966), p. 43.

9. Dom James Fox, letter to John Howard Griffin, August 28, 1971.

10. Thomas Merton, letter to John Howard Griffin, September 15, 1967.

11. Thomas Merton, note to Father John Eudes, May 4, 1967. From the files of Father John Eudes Bamberger, Abbey of Gethsemani archives.

12. Frank O'Callaghan, note to Thomas Merton, May 15, 1967. From the O'Callaghan files, Louisville, Kentucky.

13. Abbot James Fox, letter to Father Louis, July 13, 1967. Monastic archives, Abbey of Gethsemani.

14. Abbot James Fox, letter to Cardinal Koenig, August 7, 1967. Monastic archives, Abbey of Gethsemani.

15. Thomas Merton, letter to Mrs. Frank (Tommie) O'Callaghan, October 17, 1967. From the O'Callaghan files, Louisville, Kentucky.

16. Father Louis, note to Father John Eudes, October 28, 1967. From the files of Father John Eudes Bamberger, Abbey of Gethsemani archives.

17. Thomas Merton, letter to John Howard Griffin, December 8, 1967.

1968

1. Thomas Merton, *My Argument with the Gestapo* (New York: Doubleday, 1969).

2. Thomas Merton, letter to John Howard Griffin, March 27, 1968.

3. Thomas Merton, letter to John Howard Griffin, March 29, 1968.

4. John Cohen, ed. *The Essential Lenny Bruce* (New York: Ballantine, 1967).

5. Thomas Merton, letter to Lionel Landry, March 29, 1968.

6. Lawrence Schiller, *Ladies and Gentlemen: Lenny Bruce* (New York: Random House, 1974).

7. TV Premiere (NBC), November 8, 1968.

Index

Abdesalam, Sidi, 91-92, 102, 105
Ahern, Fr. Barnabas, 18, 119
Amandas, Fr., 41
American Heritage, 125
Angela of Foligno, 22
Arthron, Br. Thomas, 134
Asian Journal, The (Merton), 150
Auden, W. H., 47
Autobiography of Malcolm X, The, 111
Bachelard, G., 123
Baldwin, Fr., 32
Bamberger, Fr. John Eudes, 52, 80, 83, 97, 110, 125, 128
Baez, Joan, 68, 93
Beecher, John, 127
Bennett, Tom, 20
Bernard, Fr., 99
Berrigan, Fr. Daniel, 24, 38, 90, 111-12, 143, 147
Berrigan, Fr. Philip, 143
Berry, Wendell, 126
Bissey, Dom Columban, 99
Black Like Me (Griffin), vii-viii,
Black Priests' Caucus, 8
Bloy, Léon, 61
Boehme, Jakob, 35
Bohr, Neils, 113
Bonhoeffer, Dietrich, 106
Book of the Poor in Spirit, The, 84, 108
Boone, Andy, 21
Boyd, Fr. Malcolm, 136
Braque, George, viii
Bronowski, J., 146
Bruce, Lenny, 140-41
Bultmann, Rudolf, 26
Burns, Fr. Flavian, xii, 35, 89, 94, 106, 129, 133, 136-37
Cabaud, Jacques, 20
Cables to the Ace (Merton), 47

Camara, Dom Helder, 107, 145
Campbell, Will, 98, 114
Camus, Albert, viii, 72, 75-76, 85, 88, 89, 102, 103, 106, 111, 115, 145
Cardenal, Ernesto, 36, 46, 48
Caron, Fr. Nicholas, 117
Catholic Peace Fellowship, 37, 38, 39
Center for the Study of Nonviolence, 93
Chadwick, Nora, 25
Char, René, viii, 85
Chorlandros, St., 40
Chuang Tzu, xv, 23, 24, 48, 149, 152
Church and the Black Man, The (Griffin), 8
Clement, Br., 121
Coffield, Fr. John, 20
Collins, Mother Angela, 26
Coltrane, John, 135
Committee of Southern Churchmen, 114
Commonweal Magazine, 28
Conjectures of a Guilty Bystander (Merton), viii, 9, 35-37, 84, 97
Corman, Cid, 88
Cousins, Norman, 118
Dalai Lama, 150
Damien, Peter, 14
Dana, Doris, 97, 125
Daniel, Brad, 127
Davenport, Guy, 98, 105
Day, Dorothy, 37-38
Demetrius, St., 40
Desert Fathers, 49, 76
Devil Rides Outside, The (Griffin), vii-viii, xv
Dieckmann, Godfrey, 18
Douglass, Jim, 24, 37
Duckett, Eleanor, 25, 76

155